Hi Alyssa,

Thank you so much for requesting my first b[ook]

I hope you enjoy it

Best wishes

Chris B.

Unleash the Magnificent You!

Unleash the
Magnificent You!

*A Gazillion Ways to Turbocharge Your
Life*

Christopher Bradbury

ISBN:
Paperback: 978-1-80227-674-9
eBook: 978-1-80227-675-6
Hardback: 978-1-80227-676-3

For Clare, Scarlett and Eugenie;

for all the fun and all the wonderful moments.

Contents

INTRODUCTION

Use this book as a tool.

Thank you for buying my book. I hope you enjoy reading it as much as I've enjoyed writing it.

Why write this book?

The decision to write this book wasn't made in an instant – the idea crept up on me over a number of years. When I was 27, I left my career in technical sales and started my own telecoms business. While I'd picked up some useful experience during my fledgling sales career, I was now going it alone and pretty much making it up as I went along. I couldn't afford mentoring fees or training courses, so everything I learned from that point onwards was self-taught, either through reading business and self-help books or simply on the job through trial and error. To cut a very long story short, I managed to build the business to a point where I could sell the company and move into semi-retirement. My wife and I currently live in Sussex, England, where we're raising our two wonderful daughters.

Throughout my career I built up a library of autobiographies, business books and self-help books, and much of my reading brought a clarity of vision to my life. Why not, I thought, help others do the same? So I set out to assimilate the key points of what I've learned, and the result is this book.

A simple, practical guide

The beauty of this book lies in its simplicity. There's no jargon, padding or long anecdotes, just useful tips on how to put a plan together and get it done! I've broken down the elements of life management into small, manageable steps, incorporating ideas and exercises to help you explore your own thoughts, preferences and possibilities.

I've tried to avoid writing too much detail, but if you'd like more information, many of my sources are quoted, so you can dig a little deeper if certain subjects are particularly important to you.

My aim: to guide you to what you really want

One of the biggest lessons I've learned is that life isn't just about making more money and having loads of 'stuff'. For me it's also about fundamental human qualities such as love, integrity, passion, caring and gratitude. Each of us is unique, and I want this book to be individual to you and what you want to achieve in your life. Nobody knows you better than yourself, and through a voyage of self-discovery, I will guide you toward more of the things you want and less of the things you don't want. I will provide you with the tools to become your own life coach. We all have the capacity to understand how to live a successful, meaningful life; we just need to stop letting everything else get in the way. So be prepared to sharpen your pencil and thoroughly assess and improve your life!

In everyday life, it's easy to forget your objectives, so first I'll get you focused on your values and goals, and then we can work through the actions you need to take from there. The chapters are short but specific, and together they serve as a playbook for what you want to be and where you want to go, each one shining a light on a different facet of your life.

My aim is to help you focus on the most important questions to ask yourself, so that you can become more self-aware and certain about your life's direction and reduce the 'clutter' that stands between you and your ultimate reality. By figuring out what you really want, you can redefine what both living and loving mean to you – not in a metaphysical, abstract sense, but right here, right now, in your everyday life.

How to use this book

Each chapter of the book can be read (or reread) in isolation, so even if you pick it up and read a section at random, you'll discover useful and insightful information that will hopefully expand your perspective on that subject. That said, if you do read the book from cover to cover and follow through on the exercises, you'll reap the maximum benefit.

It's all very well learning something new, but it's only when you take action that you truly get the benefit from new information. If you want a book that requires no effort other than reading, then this isn't the book for you. You can't just read it and expect miracles to happen in your life – you have to learn the lessons and apply them to your life. The exercises and action steps throughout the book are important because they shift your thoughts outside your head and onto paper. The exercises will help you engage with the material first-hand and help you connect to your core values and discover your life purpose.

So make it a priority to follow the steps laid out within the book, reflecting and writing as you go. This will inspire you and you'll feel motivated as you achieve each step. Mark up the book with a highlighter pen, make notes or, even better, keep a journal to track your progress and collate ideas as you go.

Try This: Do a ten-day trial. If one of the ideas in this book sounds like it might work for you, try it for ten days and see if it is helpful. Ten days is a manageable chunk of time – achieve this, and you'll know you can continue for another ten days, and then another and so on.

Bon voyage!

This book isn't just a book – it's a living, breathing, organic process, facilitating a journey of self-discovery. I hope you enjoy the process; I hope you enjoy the journey; I hope you feel like you can become your own life coach; I hope you find it energising and I hope you feel inspired to move more powerfully toward your vision.

1

VALUES

The best starting point. What are your values?

What makes life worth living? Who are we and why do we do what we do? What principles guide every fibre of our being?

Psychologists split self-awareness into two types:

- **Internal self-awareness** is about recognising our value system. It's about being aware of our preferences, our motivations, our goals, our position in the world and our impact on the world.
- **External self-awareness** is about recognising how other people see us.

Research has discovered a correlation between our happiness and how self-aware we are. Those of us with high levels of internal and external self-awareness tend to make better decisions, are more effective and have deeper relationships. Your self-awareness is expressed in its purest form through the lens of your values – the chapter headings in the book of you.

Our values are unambiguous beliefs we have about what is really important and what really matters in our lives. Everyone has different values, but most of us don't consciously think about what our values are. Can you say with certainty what is most important to you? Is it love? Your health? If you're not sure, you should do a little soul-searching because the most fulfilled and happy people are those who understand their own values and live their lives accordingly. If you don't feel content with your life but you're not sure why, it could be that you're not living in accordance with your inner beliefs and values.

Identify your values

Try This: Let's begin by writing down the values that most appeal to you. To help this process and to give you more of an idea of what we mean by values, have a look at this list:

- **Achievement:** You love to achieve your goals.
- **Adventure:** You enjoy trying new things.
- **Autonomy:** You're independent and self-sufficient.
- **Boldness:** You're bold and daring. You radiate great courage.
- **Calm:** You try to handle every situation with calmness and self-control.
- **Cheerfulness:** You consciously choose to smile and be cheerful.

- **Compassion:** You relate to others with love, kindness and understanding.
- **Challenge:** You enjoy doing things that stretch you.
- **Citizenship:** You respect fellow citizens and are socially responsible.
- **Contribution:** You make a valuable contribution to the world.
- **Creativity:** You enjoy coming up with amazing new ideas.
- **Curiosity:** You're always interested in new ideas.
- **Determination:** You're persistent and determined.
- **Diversity:** You want to see an inclusive society with no one left behind.
- **Exercise:** You enjoy becoming fitter and healthier.
- **Fairness:** You seek justice and fairness in all your dealings with others.
- **Family:** You respond to your family with patience and love.
- **Freedom:** You value the freedom to do as you choose with your time.
- **Friendship:** Your friendships are meaningful and rewarding.
- **Generosity:** You share money, possessions and time.
- **Gratitude:** You express gratitude for everything you have in your life.
- **Happiness:** You seek happiness in everything you do.
- **Health:** You eat, drink, exercise and sleep well.
- **Honesty:** You live your life with honesty and truthfulness.

- **Humility:** You're modest and don't take yourself too seriously.
- **Humour:** You seek reasons to laugh because it's so much fun.
- **Inner harmony:** You endeavour to be at peace with yourself.
- **Kindness:** You strive to be kind to everyone you interact with.
- **Listening:** You know that listening to people is important and rewarding.
- **Love:** Your heart is open and you radiate love in all your relationships.
- **Loyalty:** You're loyal to the people and ideas you care about.
- **Mindfulness:** You practise mindfulness on a regular basis.
- **Optimism:** You look at the sunny side of most situations.
- **Passion:** You do things with purpose and energy.
- **Patience:** You're a tolerant and understanding person.
- **Recognition:** You like being recognised, respected and appreciated.
- **Relaxation:** You like to relax as much as possible.
- **Religion:** Your religion is very important to you.
- **Self-esteem:** You acknowledge your own self-worth.
- **Service:** You derive deep satisfaction from helping others.
- **Simplicity:** You enjoy uncluttering your environment and your life.
- **Stability:** You value stability at work and at home.
- **Success:** You work hard and enjoy the success that goes with it.

- **Wealth:** Financial prosperity is important to you.

First, choose your favourite 20 values from this list. Then choose your top 15 and then your top 10 and then your top 5. This will give you a sense of which values take priority. If you want to prioritise your list in more detail, list the values in order of importance from one to 20. If there are values that you hold dearly but they're not listed here, feel free to add them to your list. When writing down your list of values, you might want to outline how you expect to commit to them – a couple of sentences for each one should be enough.

Hopefully, you're now clearer about what is most important in your life. Establishing your values and living according to them will help you approach life's many choices with more certainty and less inner conflict.

Focus on yourself first, not others

Exploring your preferences, thoughts and emotions will hopefully lead to greater self-awareness, but be very careful not to judge yourself in the process. Choose *your* values, not someone else's. I'm not recommending that you create a value list for society as a whole, because other people have their own views which you cannot and should not attempt to control. Your values are yours and yours only. They're right for you and you only. Obviously, there will be a lot of crossover with like-minded people, but no two individuals' lists will be identical. Your values give *you* a sense of direction with which to align your actions, and together they become your personal rule book, a benchmark against which everything you do can be compared.

Also, don't choose values that you think you *should* have. At this stage refrain from asking yourself why you are the way you are and don't look for the causes of your thoughts and behaviours. Ask 'What?' not 'Why?' questions:

- What kind of person are you?
- What do you feel, think and do in given situations?

For introspection to be successful, you need to have a flexible approach: let your mind wander and explore various perspectives, but also accept that you may not immediately find definitive answers.

Consider others' values

We tend to feel mistrustful of people who have different values to our own and many disagreements are caused by contradictory value systems. Observing and understanding the values of other people in our lives enables us to appreciate why they choose what they do, which in turn enables us to understand and empathise with their decisions and actions.

Keep checking in with your values

In order to put your values into action, you need to know them well. This means reading your list once a week for four weeks and then once a month for a year. Clear values are the foundation stone for a meaningful life, so don't be tempted to skip this stage of the process. High performers challenge their own values and philosophy and ask questions all the time. This whole process will bring a certain clarity as you progress through life, which in turn will help you create more meaningful goals. Open your arms to change, but don't let go of your most heartfelt values.

Review your list every year or so to see whether you're living according to your values. If the answer is yes, that's great news. If the answer is no, then you need to adjust your life choices or adjust your list of values, or both.

Remember: Having clear values helps you think about what you really want so that you're able to fully consider your goals and then describe them more precisely. Even if you have a few million in the bank, three houses and five cars, if your lifestyle is at odds with your values, you'll be unhappy. It's vital to establish your values so you can guide, encourage and back yourself with a clarity you've never experienced before.

2

BELIEFS

Challenge your beliefs.

Consider two ladies who have just turned 70. One of these ladies thinks her life is approaching its twilight and that her best years are behind her. The other lady, however, is very excited about all the things she still wants to do. How do we explain such a massive difference in attitude? It's simply down to contrasting beliefs. The way that we view our world and ourselves is moulded by our beliefs.

What are beliefs?

Our beliefs are our ideas and observations of the world based on our life experiences. The problem is that most of us are intellectually lazy and many of our beliefs are mere generalisations, or are based on the opinions of other people. Once we adopt a belief, it usually sticks, and we hold on to our beliefs as if they're certainties. And because we're so convinced we're right, we never challenge them. As a result, many of us cling to negative beliefs that prevent us from moving in a positive direction.

Make your beliefs empowering, not limiting

Our beliefs about who we are and who we can be heavily influence who we *will* be, so if we wish to create positive changes, we need to challenge our beliefs, especially those that are working against us. For example, if we decide that something is beyond our reach, we have built a barrier. Consider the example of the two 70-year-old ladies: one thought she was too old, the other didn't. To get the most from your life, you need to swap your disabling beliefs for enabling beliefs.

Try This: For one week, make a pledge to stop criticising yourself. If you wouldn't say it to a friend, don't say it to yourself.

Don't be defined by your past

Certain things that happened in the past might not have ended well for you but be careful that they do not influence your life forever. As the years pass by, your life memories get oversimplified, and many negative memories get amplified by replaying them many times over. Try to catch yourself doing this. Learn from past experiences, but do not allow yourself to be defined by them. Your life is in the now and the future, not in the past.

Question your beliefs

Don't let your objectivity become muddled by stereotyping or by inflexible and dogmatic belief. A belief that is correct is a belief that can be substantiated with accurate data, not hearsay or random anecdotes. Unfortunately, though, most of us use poor generalisations as a proxy for hard facts; for example:

- 'All politicians are useless.'
- 'Businesses don't care about anything except making money.'
- 'I don't see myself running my own business.'
- 'I don't think I'd be any good as a manager.'

We sometimes think we're right when we're actually wrong, so from time to time we have to be willing to challenge our opinions in order to reveal our blind spots. This isn't easy because questioning our beliefs sometimes involves facing our anxieties and insecurities, or simply admitting we're wrong. Don't be deterred by this because the more we learn about ourselves and the world around us, the easier it will be to move forward.

Try This: Write down some of your most stubborn beliefs, especially the negative and less helpful ones – beliefs like 'I'm a poor parent', 'I'm usually incompetent', 'My memory is terrible' and 'I'm hopeless at XYZ'. Then challenge each belief for truth and credibility.

Follow this thought process as you challenge each belief:

1. Is the belief true, false, or somewhere in the middle?
2. What evidence is available? What feedback have I had from a range of different people?
3. Do I need to modify this belief?
4. What are the implications of the belief or modified belief being true?

This method of disputing your beliefs takes practice but is well worth doing. When challenging your beliefs in this way, you must also be realistic. For example, if you really are incompetent at a particular thing, there is no point in trying to kid yourself that you're not. In these situations, you need to decide how important your incompetence is. If it's not that important, then try to work around it or if it's really important then make a plan to become more competent. If a belief isn't useful, you need to train yourself to let it go, change it or just reduce its intensity.

Remember: To initiate a transformation in your life you must begin by challenging your beliefs. Abandon false beliefs that work against you and replace them with realistic and empowering beliefs that help you get where you want to be.

3

OPTIMISM

If the glass is half-empty, let's make it half-full.

Are you an optimist or a pessimist or somewhere in between? If you think you're an optimist, how do you know you are? Are you just calling yourself an optimist because you think that it's better than calling yourself a pessimist? Sometimes we think we're optimistic but we still harbour a sizeable percentage of negative or pessimistic thoughts.

Optimists and pessimists come in all guises and it's often not easy to categorise people unless we know them very well. There are, however, two main tendencies that pessimists and optimists have. When faced with a problem or difficult situation:

- **An optimist considers it a one-off, whereas a pessimist thinks the setback is part of a more enduring problem.** For example, if you apply and then fail to get a new job, you might think, 'I never get the jobs I really want.' By using the word 'never', you make the setback permanent and you might give up. An optimist, however, will interpret the same outcome as an isolated event: 'I didn't get this job, but I'll soon get another one.'

- **An optimist thinks outside factors caused the issue, whereas pessimists blame themselves.** For example, if a pessimist loses a tennis match, they'll think 'I'm not good enough' or 'I made too many errors'. An optimist, on the other hand, will externalise the defeat and put it down to superior play from their opponent.

Depending on their life experiences, some people become pessimists, thinking they have little control over their destiny, and some people become optimists, feeling a strong sense of self-empowerment over what lies ahead. Most of us find a place somewhere in between.

Our thinking habits are learned during childhood, mainly from parents, caregivers, schoolteachers and friends. Children usually imitate their parents' behaviour, so if a parent tends to explain events optimistically, their child will be more likely to develop a similar habit. However, because our internal dialogue is learned, we can relearn and change the way we 'talk' to ourselves. Therefore, if you've acquired a pessimistic outlook in childhood, you're not predestined to have it forever. This is good news because there are many reasons why it's preferable to be an optimist.

Reasons to be optimistic

Optimistic people set more difficult goals and put in more effort to attain those goals than their pessimistic counterparts. Optimists are generally healthier, they have a stronger immune system, they're more likely to take good care of themselves and they feel they have fewer negative life events than pessimists, resulting in lower levels of stress. Optimistic people find it easier to make friends and keep friends.

Given identical levels of talent, optimists are more likely to win at sports competitions. This is mainly down to increased levels of confidence, as pessimists are rarely confident of their abilities, especially after a prior defeat.

Children with an optimistic outlook do better in the classroom than their pessimistic peers and optimistic college students generally achieve better grades. Optimists tend to thrive in most work environments too, especially in jobs that involve a lot of risk and rejection, such as sales and telemarketing.

Life is often about confronting and solving problems. When a pessimist encounters a major challenge, they're likely to resign themselves to failure and admit defeat at the first sign of trouble. Optimists see setbacks as a challenge, and instead of giving up, they try harder and attempt to rise above even the most hopeless situations. In a similar way pessimism, unfortunately, promotes depression. While loss, defeat and failure are major causes of depression, this will be magnified if a person believes that they can do nothing to change the situation – they believe their actions will be pointless.

Your happiness largely depends on how you interpret the world around you. How you feel isn't directly caused by events in your life, it's the product of your evaluation of those events. Successful people tend to search for possibilities and positive outcomes in any given situation. Even when faced with numerous setbacks, they cut through the doom and gloom and plough on, always thinking in terms of opportunities.

If you're an optimist, that's great, but if you're a pessimist or somewhere in the middle, the good news is that you can train your brain to become much more optimistic.

Challenge your thinking

Try This: Most of our self-talk is unconscious and so begin by observing your inner dialogue, especially in the midst of negative events. Specifically, look out for these pessimistic tendencies:

- Are you interpreting that single setback as a sign of complete failure?
- How quickly do you give up on a task?
- Are you overgeneralising in a negative way? Does this 'always' happen to you, are you 'always' unlucky?

Keep on the lookout for clues and analyse your thought processes, especially if these are pessimistic. It's impossible to do this 100 per cent of the time, but keep trying nevertheless, as some feedback is better than none.

Also, pay attention to other people's comments and patterns of behaviour. Spotting optimists and pessimists around you will give further clues about how you can become more optimistic.

Try This: Begin to question your thought processes and belief systems. Focus on the specifics of each scenario as it arises and try to avoid generalising in a negative way. If your train of thought is pessimistic, challenge it!

If, like many people, you find it difficult to challenge your own opinions, get a close friend to do the exercise with you. Ask them to attack your negative beliefs about yourself or the situation you're in.

Three positive things

Try This: To direct your focus towards optimism, each morning write down three positive things that happened the day before. These can be simple things like a funny incident, a small job well done or a positive connection with someone.

This might be hard to do every day at first, but keep going. This little exercise will train your mind to be on the lookout for positive experiences, which will increase the quality of your day and hopefully the quality of your life.

Look for the good

In life, we find what we want to find. If you seek out unpleasantness in the world, you'll easily find it. If you want to find mistakes that people make, you'll undoubtedly be able to find them. Instead, proactively seek positive events and experiences because the more positivity your brain is exposed to, the more optimistic you'll become. Limit your exposure to 'bad' news and current affairs and instead seek out success stories wherever and whenever you can.

Observe positive people. There is a lightness about them. They've learned not to take themselves too seriously and they're a joy to be around. Look out for solid, positive people and include these people more and more in your life. Observe the wider world and search for the minor miracles of daily life – a beautiful sunset, a magnificent tree or a friendly smile.

Words have power

Try This: Adopt an optimist's vocabulary. The words and phrases that we attach to our experiences can become our experiences, so by changing the way we describe it, we can change the intensity of an experience. For example, if you describe a wonderful experience as being 'all right', the intensity of it will be diminished by your choice of words. Listen to what you're saying out loud and try whenever possible to raise the intensity a notch or two. For example, change 'good' to 'excellent', or 'like' to 'love', or 'nice' to 'fantastic'. In a similar vein, try to lower the intensity of your negative words, so 'livid' or 'angry' become 'disappointed' or 'surprised', and 'I hate' becomes 'I prefer'. Experiment with some new words and expressions until you find a few that you feel comfortable with.

Also, try to take the edge off your irritation by using rare or funny words. You could even try to make yourself and those around you smile. For example, when you're particularly angry, you could say, 'I must say I feel quite miffed!'

Ignore your negative chatterbox

Negative self-talk is one of the most destructive aspects of the human psyche. We're always going to have negative thoughts, but we do have a choice about how we process them. We can either let them upset us or we can learn to not take them so seriously.

Tune in to your inner dialogue regularly and try to establish whether it's positive or negative. Is it helping you or hindering you? Is it making you happy or unhappy? When your inner dialogues veer toward the negative, maybe it's time to challenge them, or even dismiss them completely, freeing up more mind space for positivity.

Distance yourself from negative thoughts

One common thinking trap is 'black or white' thinking, which involves classifying events into extremes or blowing them out of proportion. For example, a situation doesn't have to be either 'perfect' or 'messed up'; it can be many things in between. Your thoughts craft and design your experiences, so use them wisely. Try to be optimistic. Learn from your mistakes, don't wallow in them. Strive to search for the positives and strive even harder to search for solutions.

Remember: Raw talent isn't that useful unless it's matched with optimism. Optimists are normally cheerful, happy and popular, and they're resilient in adapting to failures and hardship. Optimists take risks, make changes and get things done. Super-optimists are the creative trailblazers and leaders of all aspects of our society. Their confidence in positive outcomes helps them get resources from others. It raises the morale of everyone around them and maximises their prospects of success. When action is required, optimism is most definitely a good thing!

4

GROWTH

Widen your horizons. Open your mind and grow, Grow, GROW!

Do you have a rigid mind or an open mind? Here's a look at what life is like with these two mindsets:

- **People with a rigid mind** believe they're naturally talented at doing some things and naturally incompetent at doing other things. They label themselves, other people and other entities as being good or bad at something. They have all the answers and do not listen to other people's opinions.

- **People with an open mind** think they can improve at virtually anything if they put the necessary effort in. As a result, they continue growing throughout their lives, acquiring new skills and actively seeking new opportunities and connections. They remove self-imposed limitations and recognise their ability to grow and improve, to accept failures and roadblocks, to learn new methods and to learn from experts in their chosen field. They listen to other people's opinions and try to learn from them.

How do these totally opposite mindsets develop? Well, it begins the minute a new baby is born. The baby enters the world with a growth mindset and then the adults in the child's environment – predominantly parents – play a massive part in maintaining this mindset or not. Children are instinctively curious, often asking questions: Where does snow come from? Why are tigers stripy? How do aeroplanes stay in the air? This inbuilt curiosity leads to constant learning, which expands their understanding of the world. Open minded parents encourage their children to continue learning by trial and error, whereas those with a rigid mind tend to judge and criticise their children, constantly emphasising to them what is good or bad and right or wrong, with little room available for error or failure.

Most of us don't live at the extremes of these two mindsets but if you've developed a leaning toward a rigid mind, you can change if you put some effort in.

Expand your mind

If you have a rigid mind, firstly recognise that you want validation, not truth. You want to hear things that make you feel good and give you comfort about who or where you are right now. Maintaining the status quo feels comfortable, and movement feels scary, risky and demanding. But just because you *believe* you're right, that doesn't mean you *are* right.

Try This: Consciously develop an enthusiasm to try new things. Make an effort to read articles or books with different points of view. You don't need to change your central values; all you're doing is expanding and developing your mind and exposing it to new ideas.

Everyone feels their own ideas are sound and worth listening to, but when an opinion conflicts with the opinion of a rigid minded person, that person will find ways to pick holes in it. And the result is they learn nothing! Most viewpoints have some positive aspects, but these will be missed if we only go looking for mistakes. In future, when someone offers an opinion that's different to yours, rather than criticise and rebut it, see if you can see it from their side, or at the least try to discover something new. This is the essence of learning.

Avoid labels

In constructing our reality, the human mind loves to put things into categories, and these can include stereotypes. Racism, for example, exists because of racial stereotypes that our brains interpret as reality. Sexism, homophobia and many other forms of intolerance come down to negative categorising and stereotyping in the brain.

To adopt an open mind, you need to use your brain more intelligently and look beyond labels. Try not to let your objectivity be muddled by rigid beliefs and labels. By clinging to inflexible and outdated opinions, you'll miss out on all sorts of possibilities, discoveries and insights.

Try This: Write down a few of your long held dogmatic beliefs – those you've always taken for granted. See if you can unpick them by arguing against them. Ask new questions and the answers will help you seek out new ways of looking at things.

Reach out to others – and listen

When listening to others, think carefully about what they're saying before rushing to judgement. Attentive listening is about being willing to understand other people's ideas and opinions without applying your own filters. Practising this skill will help you open both your heart and your mind and challenge your preconceived notions of the world.

With a willing spirit and an open mind, you'll establish more fruitful, co-operative interactions with work colleagues, friends and loved ones. Be particularly willing to learn from family and friends. The individuals closest to us know and understand us the most and can often offer very intuitive ideas.

Remember: We often hang out with people who think like us, which minimises our exposure to a diversity of thoughts and beliefs. But when there's no variety of ideas, there's essentially only one idea – and that will not help drive positive change.

New and varied opinions, on the other hand, will lead to new and varied opportunities to learn and grow. Over time, as you engage with different perspectives, you'll build compassion for yourself and for others, and you'll become more philosophical. Take the shackles off, keep an open mind, and let your curiosity take over.

5

CALLING

What excites you? Do you have a calling?

When most people go to work, they are motivated by outside influences like cash, status or reputation, but achieving any of these things doesn't always make us any happier. True happiness usually emanates from contributing to a higher purpose – contributing to something that is greater than ourselves. Work that correlates strongly with our passions, principles, goals and philosophy will no longer feel like work.

In a study from Johns Hopkins University, students were questioned about the things they thought were fundamental to their lives. Nearly 80 per cent stated that discovering a meaning and purpose in life was key to their happiness. People who do not live according to their values, or feel that their lives have little meaning, often feel a nagging emptiness inside.

Unfortunately, many people have no idea what they want from life. They zigzag about without a life ambition or a clear sense of purpose, often leading an unfulfilled life where they simply do what their peers are doing or what their parents want them to do. While this strategy might pay the bills in the short term, it holds people back from taking risks and finding meaning in their lives.

Ikigai

The people living on the remote Japanese island of Okinawa realise that meaning and purpose are vital factors for happiness. Okinawans are blessed with the longest human lifespan on the planet, yet they rarely retire from work in their later years. Instead, they have *ikigai*. There is no direct English translation, but it's a word that symbolises the concept of taking joy from everyday living. Essentially, ikigai is the reason you get up in the morning and Okinawans see this as crucial to their sense of well-being.

Researchers at Tohoku University showed that those with *ikigai* had lower stress, were healthier, had longer lifespans and generally reported that they were doing fulfilling activities each day.

Ikigai has been described as a coming together of four components:

- Do what you love
- Do what you're good at
- Do something you can be paid for
- Do something the world needs

Many Japanese people believe that we all have an *ikigai*, or 'calling', that we are born to do, and if our *ikigai* is our career, we should never take early retirement. If their *ikigai* is a hobby that brings happiness, Okinawans keep partaking throughout their later years.

A true calling is an activity that intertwines the essential characteristics of *ikigai*: your passions, your skills, how you earn money and what the world needs.

Try This: Think of an activity that appeals to you. The activity could be a major hobby or, better still, a potential career. Then ask yourself these questions:

- Is this activity important to you or is it meaningful? The answer may not be immediately obvious, so it's worth giving this some thought.
- Is this activity enjoyable?
- Is this activity something you're good at or is it something that you know you could become good at?

One secret to leading a happy life is to participate in as many activities as possible that satisfy these conditions. If any of these activities is a possible career option, then you might have hit the jackpot. This could be your calling!

A different path ahead?

When we're young and considering our career opportunities at school or college, we're encouraged to do what we're good at, as opposed to what inspires us or what we might enjoy. Even if you do find a job you enjoy, but you employer doesn't share your values and philosophy, you could easily end up feeling unfulfilled and demotivated

Try This: Give this matter some deep thought. Is there an alternative career path or major lifestyle choice that could be your true calling? It could be that you feel triumphant when you find a beautiful piece of art? Perhaps you get excited when you see a classic car, or when you're absorbed in doing something creative or doing something outdoors. Think of an experience or a time when you were really committed to something. What were the consequences of that commitment? More importantly, what are you committed to now? When an activity fully consumes your attention, it's a great clue as to what your calling might be.

A year to live?

Try This: You might find some clues by considering your mortality. What would you do with your time if you discovered you would die in exactly one year? If nothing else, this exercise will make you aware of how you're spending your time generally and how much of your time isn't being spent doing things that give you joy, meaning or purpose.

If you get stuck...

Another person with a fresh perspective can be a valuable resource in identifying your inner motivations. This person doesn't need to be in your inner circle, just someone who's interested and perceptive. Try to find someone who will ask provocative questions – your answers might provide useful indicators and expose strong feelings. Together, explore your most formative and memorable stories – these are an important part of the discovery process.

Remember: Don't worry if you can't immediately identify your calling. You might not even have one, or you may not be 100 per cent sure of the things that are important to you. Have a think about this while you work through this book and keep an eye out for signposts pointing you toward the type of activities that have meaning for you.

6

FLOW

What do you love doing? Find your flow.

If you're struggling to find out if you have a calling or not (see Chapter 5), it might help to think instead about those moments when you experience the feeling of 'flow'. This phenomenon has been extensively researched by the psychologist Mihaly Csikszentmihalyi. Flow occurs when we become totally absorbed by something. Whether it's doing something creative, practising an instrument, playing a sport, or even completing an interesting task at work: we're so captivated that time flies by and distractions simply go unnoticed. This state of flow releases us from our self-consciousness, worries and anxieties – we experience complete engagement and happiness in that moment. For these reasons finding our flow is deeply satisfying and pleasurable.

From a very early age we often do what others expect us to do, and we eventually find a job that makes our parents proud or impresses our peer group. We may be unhappy, unfulfilled or feel trapped, but we don't break out because we fear losing the approval we've worked so hard for. Deep down, however, there are doubts. Is this really what I want? Should I be doing something else? We long for self-realisation, to follow our calling, to find our flow, but instead of changing course we look for positives in the status quo, and we end up convincing ourselves that we're content.

But is it possible to live another way? Is it possible to live a life unconstrained by other people's expectations?

What puts you in the flow?

When you're in the flow state, you become fully immersed and fully involved in an activity. You have an increased belief in your capabilities and a feeling of energised focus. Most people report that being in a state of flow is deeply satisfying.

Try This: When have you experienced this? Take a step back and think about activities that you love to immerse yourself in. These can be activities you do now or have done in the past. Don't judge the activities; simply identify them. Keep a 'flow log' in which you note the activities that keep you engaged, energetic and in a state of flow.

Please yourself

Getting yourself into a true state of flow is rarely motivated by cash incentives or outside approval. These things may or may not be added benefits, but the main reward is based on pleasing you and you alone. It's about enjoying the process.

Many specialists such as scientists, artists and architects have achieved great things purely because they enjoyed the challenge of refining their specific skills and pushing boundaries. Albert Einstein, for example, worked by day in a Swiss patent office while formulating his scientific theories during his leisure time.

Work at a comfortable level

When setting out to experience a state of flow, it's important to establish the optimum level of difficulty. If you choose an activity that's far too easy, you'll get bored. If you choose an activity that's far too difficult, you'll get frustrated and demotivated. If you operate at a level of competency you can enjoy, your flow will come naturally and effortlessly. Whenever we engage in something that's neither too easy nor too difficult, we expand our personal limits and achieve more.

If you're a beginner at tennis, for example, you'll initially enjoy trying to hit the ball against a wall and simply keep the ball moving. As you improve, this might start to bore you and you'll start looking to challenge yourself by playing against someone else. If your opponent is too good, you'll soon feel uncomfortable and out of your depth, but if your opponent is just a little better, you'll remain roughly within your comfort zone yet be sufficiently challenged to improve your skills.

Try new things

Push yourself out of your comfort zone and try as many new things as possible. Find out more about those things you've always been curious about but have never tried. Maybe meet new people and travel more? Who knows what passions you might have that are waiting to be discovered?

Remember: Seeking out activities that produce a flow-like state will increase your enjoyment of your time here on Earth. If your life is full of 'flow', you will know you are following your own authentic path, and you will be more motivated and fulfilled.

7

GOALS

Where are you going? What are your goals?

Assuming that you're aware of your values (see Chapter 1) and have given some thought to when you feel flow (Chapter 6) and what your calling could be (Chapter 5), now is a great moment to assess your goals.

Start with a blank page and have some fun juggling around a few new ideas. Use this time to go off-script and consider some weird and wacky ideas as well as the relatively obvious and conventional ideas about how to live your life.

Who are you?

How deeply have you thought about this? Who do you think you are? Why do you do the things that you do? To some extent, we all adhere to the stereotypes we've given ourselves, so for the time being, forget the past. Who are you now and who will you be in the future? Write down all the fundamental aspects of your character you already have. Then write down some aspects that you would like to have. Be honest, but be bold and adventurous with this!

Brainstorm

Think about your career. Is your job enjoyable? Or is it dull? Should you look for a new job doing a similar role, or should you change direction and start a completely new career? Or maybe move to a different location?

Try This: When choosing suitable careers, people tend to focus solely on their work or study experience to date. To broaden your horizons, make a list of all your strengths, then write down lots of job options that fit with those strengths. The more you can think of, the better. What exactly is your dream job? And why aren't you doing it?

Ask similar questions about everything else in your life:

- Your relationships
- Your hobbies
- Your leisure time
- Your diet
- Your exercise regime
- Where you live
- Where you go on holiday

Everything is up for grabs, so try not to discount anything at this stage – just dream a little and follow your heart. Ask yourself: what do I really want in life? And why do I want these things?

The more ideas, the better

At the Stanford Graduate School of Education, Professor Dan Schwartz observed that people who have many ideas for problem solving are more likely to discover creative solutions than people who come up with only one or two. So keep those ideas coming. And coming. And coming!

Review your life so far and assess your happiness at different times. What does this tell you? What guidance would you give yourself? Adopt the attitude of a novice and start asking the type of questions a complete beginner would ask. Do some research on the internet or make a few phone calls. Your thinking needs to be flexible but focused, so keep drilling down with 'Why?', 'What?' and 'How?' questions. What is success for you? How will this make you happy? These questions are worth spending some time on – they are the signposts on your road of discovery. This is your life, so move it closer to what you want it to be.

You need to know so much about what you desire that whenever you're going toward it, you know it and feel it with every sinew in your body.

See your goals and experience them in your mind and heart. Play movies of you doing what you'd love to do. Are these movies realistic? If the answer is yes, step inside the movies and enjoy being in various stages of the story. Visualise yourself living out a scene that excites you and puts a huge smile on your face. Let the feelings flow and enjoy it. Do this regularly.

Aim to be a good person

Take the time to add in a few behavioural goals that support your values and philosophy. By this I mean goals related to traits such as kindness, humility, compassion and generosity – whatever appears on your list of desirable values.

What kind of person are you and what kind of person do you want be? Are you kind to other people? Are you kind to other creatures and the planet? Are you kind to yourself? Do you easily get hot under the collar or are you patient and composed? Are you a generous person? Are you a grateful person? While it's great to own lots of nice things and to have a few notable accomplishments under your belt, your happiness will also depend heavily on these character traits and how you communicate with yourself at the deepest level.

List your goals

Having spent a few days coming up with some ideas, write them all down. Only three per cent of people write down their goals and these people achieve five to ten times as much as the other 97 per cent.

Now you have a list of possible goals. Some goals will be easy and some difficult; some will be short and sweet, and some will be years in the making. It's time to analyse the list and decide which are viable and achievable, and which have the highest priority (for more on prioritising, see Chapter 8).

Before we go through this process, however, I'd like to get you up to date with the latest research on goal setting and how our goals relate to our overall happiness.

Goal-setting 101

We must be a little careful with some of our goals. Sometimes the pleasure derived from goal achievement can be short-lived. We might think a new house or new car will make us happy, but these goals often lead to a small spike in our level of happiness. Once we acquire the new house or the new car, there's every chance that we'll soon be looking for the next new house or car that's bigger, better or faster. And on and on the cycle repeats, so that we're never really satisfied with what we have.

Try not to set goals that are entirely based on impressing other people – the only person you need to impress is yourself. Instead, think about goals that will leave you feeling truly fulfilled within. For example, your goals do not have to be about money, possessions or your reputation. Some of the happiest people on the planet have nothing.

Pleasure is a desirable state that we associate with the pursuit of happiness. For sustainable happiness, however, we need something else. As we've discovered in previous chapters, a truly fulfilling life depends on combining pleasure with meaning. This is the secret to attaining true happiness. Taking drugs might be an extremely pleasurable experience in that moment, but it can't produce true happiness because there is no meaning, and we need meaning to make it fulfilling.

We must therefore search for activities and experiences that elicit enjoyable emotions but are also meaningful to us on a deeper level. Only when our goals satisfy these principles will they truly yield long-term happiness.

Consider an accountant who feels fulfilled in his career and happy because he is interested in accountancy. Strangely enough, he might have a more meaningful, pleasurable and fulfilling life than a teacher who joined the profession because of pressure from his parents. One study found that 85 per cent of millennials want a career with a purpose and one that benefits the world, not just themselves.

It's also important to enjoy the journey. Think back to when you've pursued and completed a goal, but you were left feeling unfulfilled. These types of goals aren't in accordance with your true desires, so drop them. Goals that you dread aren't worth chasing either. For example, there's no point in spending hundreds of hours learning a new language or learning to play a new instrument if the very process of that learning gives you zero pleasure.

Try This: What goals in your past have led to an enjoyable and fulfilling outcome? Now look into the future – what goals do you think will create similar positive outcomes going forward? Recall your most notable life events, both good and bad. This will help you understand what brings joy to your life. Also make a note of those 'flow' moments when you became entirely engrossed in an activity and time just flew by.

Another clue is your energy levels. Some activities sap your energy, but others can raise your energy levels. For example, if you feel tired and bored sitting in a health and safety meeting but feel energised after a sales meeting with a potential customer, this might be a useful indicator. Also keep in mind that a goal shouldn't force you to compromise on the things that really matter to you, such as special relationships and activities that you love.

Planning for success

You should now have a long list of possibilities. Unless your list is very short and specific, I doubt you'll be able to do or achieve everything on that list, and if you set too many goals and try to do too many things at once, you may get demotivated, which is obviously counterproductive. Your motivation levels need to remain high so that you can circumnavigate the roadblocks and setbacks that will surely arise as you execute your plan. So evaluate the options and narrow them down to a list of goals that one person can achieve in one lifetime.

Feel free to have big, ambitious goals, but make sure they're realistic. Overconfident planning, sometimes referred to as 'planning fallacy', is one of the main threats to goal attainment. Planning fallacy was a phrase first coined by psychologists Amos Tversky and Daniel Kahneman. They discovered that people very often miscalculate how long it takes to get things done. So if we begin goals with excessive expectations, this will lead to more frustration and impatience, which will eventually lead to simply giving up.

Here's a couple of simple and reliable ways to avoid this planning fallacy:

- **Reduce the number of goals on your list by 50%, or reduce each goal by 50%, or both.** This will reduce the probability of giving up due to taking on too many things at once.

- **Break up a large goal into smaller milestones.** This makes it easier to achieve because you stay motivated as you regularly complete each small step. The pleasure you get from earning a reward is related to the dopamine your brain releases when you anticipate that reward, so just the thought of checking off a meaningful goal is treated as a reward in your brain. It's therefore more motivating to set small and frequent mini goals, which create regular dopamine rewards, than it is to just aim for a single large and distant goal.

Motivation is key to achieving goals, so incorporate it in your planning. Here are a few ideas:

- **Mix your personal goal with an external obligation to benefit others.** If your choice of charity will benefit as a result of your project's success, you might work harder to ensure it comes together.

- **Share your goal with a few other people.** No one wishes to be seen to fail, so the more people who know what you're doing, the more committed you'll feel. This technique is not for everyone as the external pressure might cause an extra layer of stress, which some people might find demotivating. That said, it's generally useful to have people around you who support your goals. It's also very useful to connect with and spend time with people who have similar goals to yours.

- **Commit publicly.** On the website Stickk.com, you can introduce a layer of peer pressure to your goals by signing a commitment contract. After signing up on the website, users state their goal with a specific deadline and have the option to stake money on their success. If they achieve their goal, they get their money back, but if they fail, the money goes to the person or organisation they selected at the outset. Sharing your goals with the world in this way will push you harder to commit to them.

Remember: Once you decide a goal is a priority, give it tremendous emotional intensity and focus. Then, hopefully, any idea or resource that supports its attainment will eventually become clear. Review your list of major goals every week and check your full list of goals every month. You values and aspirations will change over time, so add new goals to both lists as they crop up and remove any goals that become redundant. Use new goals to establish new routines and new opportunities. Use them to Unleash the Magnificent You!

8

PRIORITIES

You can't do everything. What are your priorities?

Imagine you're at the twilight of your life, looking back. Do you wish your priorities had been different? Do you wish you'd spent more time with people and on activities you truly loved and less time doing things that really didn't matter that much? Look back at your life now while you still have the opportunity to make some changes. Then look forward and begin to make those changes.

We can easily feel overwhelmed when we try to do too many things at once, so it's helpful to keep asking ourselves, 'What's really important?' We have many responsibilities, but we have a choice about where we allocate the greatest amount of energy: family time, exercise, leisure, hobbies, reading, holidays and making a living. Answering this question will help you align your actions with your values and goals.

Try This: Make a list of the most important aspects of your life and begin to make plans to allocate more of your time to the items on that list. This process might involve many moving parts and interdependencies, so it might be less daunting if you address one aspect of your life at a time. As soon as you've mastered one area, you'll gain momentum which will help give you the confidence to address other areas.

It's okay to quit and to say no

Many of us at some point or another have been trapped in demotivating jobs and failing relationships. As we grow up, we're told that giving up is a bad thing and that we should 'stick with the programme' and never quit. It can therefore be difficult to put an end to what we don't like, so we tolerate things that waste our time or make us unhappy. It simply isn't feasible to do everything or to enjoy everything, so try to view quitting as necessary and normal. If it's obvious that something isn't working out, don't waste any more time on it.

Have you ever attended a social or business engagement that you didn't really want to go to? Occasionally, you will have to attend, but unless you really, *really* must go to the event, you'd be truer to yourself by not going. Make your own decisions and choose to do things that *you* want to do, not what others expect you to do. Be protective of your time and learn when to say no. If you tend to say 'I have to' rather than 'I want to', you're surrendering your power to choose and giving others permission to choose for you.

People tend to fear saying no. They feel it would be socially uncooperative and they feel pressured not to disappoint the people around them. If this sounds like you, just remember that your relationships should not depend on you saying yes to everything. If they do, then something is wrong. Saying no may cause a moment of guilt as you fret about someone else's disappointment, but being true to yourself will pay handsome dividends in the long run. If, for example, your family is your top priority, you shouldn't be wasting your free time doing favours for casual acquaintances instead of spending it with your children.

Subtly make sure other people understand that your time is limited and be clear about your priorities. If we say 'no' more often, we'll upset people much less than we might imagine, and the people around us will quickly work out that we simply don't have time or the desire to do everything asked of us.

Put your favourite people at the top of the list

Dedicating more time to your central relationships and your favourite people has obvious benefits. These people are fun and easy to be around so enjoy their company as much as you can.

Remember: Analyse what you've done in the past and use this analysis to avoid going down paths that have nothing to offer. Rigorously prioritise everything you do so that you always take care of the important things first and deal with everything else later. Regularly give yourself time and space to see the bigger picture and think clearly about what needs to be done and what is most important. Free yourself from all the people and things that add zero value to your life. Prioritising in this way will improve your sense of joy and well-being and make each day just that little bit more enjoyable!

9

LIFE MANAGEMENT

Be your own life manager.

'You only get one life' may be a cliché but it's also absolutely true. You get one life only and it's all yours, so you shouldn't live it any other way than what suits you and those that care about you. Many of us are masterminds at contriving justifications to sidestep change in our lives, but people who know what they want don't just wait to see what life throws up; they proactively design their lifestyle, and you need to do the same – it's time to take charge and manage your life.

Visualise your ideal life

To begin, you need to build a vision. To live the life you want, you can't be too vague or ambiguous; you need a sharply focused vision of your life. When you picture a perfect period of time, relaxing images of holidays and leisure activities might pop up, but this process is really about creating a day, a week or a year that contains all that's truly important to you, including things that will help you to reach your goals.

Try This: Visualise an ideal day from when you wake up to when you go to bed:

- Where are you today?
- Who are you spending time with today?
- What are you doing in the morning? In the afternoon? In the evening?
- Who are you eating with?
- Where are you going to work and how do you get there? Or are you in a house on a mountain settling in to spend the day working from home?

Also try mapping out an ideal week using a blank week planner. Visualise seven perfect days, accounting for work, weekend and leisure time. This process will give you a clear idea of what you truly want and hopefully will inspire you and motivate you to move forward with your goals straightaway.

With a clear vision, solid motivation and a strong understanding of your priorities (see Chapter 8), you'll begin to see that you can live your ideal life. It just takes some perseverance, a high level of commitment, some positive thinking and a firm belief in yourself.

Manage your life and manage it well

Demand more of yourself in all aspects of your life: your appearance, health, interactions with others, interactions with yourself, time management, work performance and overall level of happiness. Begin each day with the question, 'How can I improve my life today?'

Beware that silent killer of well-laid plans, procrastination, and use your strategy, planning and execution to overcome it. Willpower alone is usually not enough, so identify those events, habits and situations that set you up for failure. (Chapter 12 has more guidance on dealing with procrastination.)

Make yourself accountable

If you're sad, angry, dissatisfied or confused, deal with the issue – which might require an honest discussion, an apology or simple forgiveness. Don't hang on to this kind of baggage; instead try to give yourself emotional closure. People who avoid personal accountability are effectively passing responsibility to others. They make lame excuses, blame others, lie to themselves and fail to seize the initiative to change their life circumstances. So make personal accountability a habit:

- See issues as they arise. Own them and tackle them.
- Identify your own poor performance, so you can make adjustments and improvements.

- Don't deny or disregard your mistakes but analyse them and work out what went wrong.
- Encourage feedback from others and act on it.
- Encourage feedback from yourself. For example, at the end of each day ask yourself:
  o How has today added to my quality of life?
  o What changes can I make to improve things?

When you ask yourself questions such as these, always try to frame them as active and not passive questions. For example, 'Was I happy today?' is a passive question, whereas 'Did I make an effort to be happy today?' is an active question. In this way we subtly force ourselves to focus more on what we actively make happen as opposed to what passively happens to us.

Be adaptable

Although planning is very useful, you don't need to stick with a plan if it isn't working. Also, keep in mind that you're not responsible for everything and you can't change all situations. Adapt your plans to your changing needs and interests – you haven't signed a contract saying you'll do the same thing for your entire life.

You'll always encounter testing times, but negative events only upset you when your expectations aren't met, so keep your expectations realistic and don't be afraid to move the goalposts when problems arise. The road to success isn't always a fast straight road – it often involves narrow winding lanes and diversions along the way.

Remember: It's time to start living your dreams right now – not tomorrow or next week or next year. Challenge your doubts. Challenge yourself to do something that frightens you on a regular basis. Living a happy life means being prepared to do difficult things and to have difficult discussions. It means looking beyond the conventional. Act now and live each day to the max!

10

PASSION

Crank up the intensity. Show me the passion!

Do the people closest to you see you as passionate, someone who puts their all into life? If the answer is no, that's a signal that you're holding something back. All successful people have a stimulating, energising and all-consuming passion that drives them to take action and to grow. Passion gives their lives excitement and meaning in a more sustainable way than simple hedonistic pleasure.

Living a life that we love quite simply means doing what we love as often as possible. We can't live the life we love when we're dominated by fears, worry and regret. When you live each minute of each day because of who you are deep inside, you will have discovered your passion in life and your energy and enthusiasm will shine through. Research demonstrates that people with passion in their lives are healthier, better sleepers and more relaxed.

As we grow and mature and our life situation evolves, we need to find new motivations to keep our passion fresh. For example, your career will consist of a string of goals, each one more daring than the previous one. When you're passionate about your career, you approach each task with total engagement and focus. When you retire, rather than do nothing, you adjust your goals to give you a lifestyle that makes you happy, motivated and fulfilled.

If we're passionate about life, we're fully absorbed in everything we do. We're interested, stimulated, excited and engaged. If we get involved in an activity that's relatively dull or tedious, we try to bring some meaning to it. As you become more adept at doing this, you will discover that you can add enthusiasm to any endeavour because that's the way you've decided to approach life.

Try to live life in the present moment and really value every day that's given to you. Passion will turn any challenge, no matter how mundane, into an opportunity. Passion will diminish apathy, and when you face rejection or similar setbacks, your passion will keep you going.

Remember: Passion is unbridled enthusiasm to move our lives onward with an upbeat attitude. If we speak with more conviction and move our bodies in a way that demonstrates excitement, our passion will naturally follow. When you're asked how you're feeling, do you often say, 'Okay thank you'? Is 'okay' really how you want to feel? Why aren't you 'good' or 'brilliant'? Become thrilled and energised by what you're doing and move toward your goals with fun and excitement. Inspire others to be the same. Now is the time to unleash your passion and allow it to influence and shape your life for the better!

11

ACTION

No more excuses. It's time for action!

The greatest advantage that successful people have over the average person is their willingness to take action. Life rewards action!

To take action, you need to:

- **Be conscientious**, which means you get things done. That means ploughing through to-do lists and sticking to your schedule as much as possible.
- **Avoid procrastination**, which only holds you back in life (more on this in Chapter 12).
- **Take responsibility**, which means you have the power to change the scenario and determine the outcome.
- **Be proactive** and make things happen.

The last point is especially important. We all have the capacity to be proactive, but many people still prefer to be reactive and allow external circumstances to dictate their behaviour, emotions and outcomes. Reactive people complain and worry about things they can't alter. Proactive people not only work on things within their control but also work hard to influence wider issues that are important to them. Reactive people avoid any kind of struggle, but proactive people learn how to greet challenges with a smile. It's all about having the right attitude, and rather than complaining about life being hard, proactive people see each new challenge as an opportunity to grow.

Be bold

Often all we need to do is just take that first step, but instead we dilly-dally and search for reasons not to. Our heads go round in circles with endless questions of self-doubt: 'Am I ready for this?'; 'What if this or that goes wrong?' If we're not careful, months can turn into years, which can turn into a lifetime of paralysis.

I'm not suggesting that we shouldn't research and plan carefully before we decide to pursue a project, but we'll never get anywhere sitting on the fence. The only way to test your ideas is to get off your backside and get to work. If you hesitate because you don't think you're quite ready, or the time isn't quite right, or your idea isn't quite perfect, or for any other excuse under the sun, you may never begin, so make that first step and get started.

The best way to build your skills is to plough through your task list. You'll develop new skills on the job and build your self-confidence when things go well. Setbacks will undoubtedly occur but push through those one by one as you head toward your goal. Whatever the result, you'll feel energised by the simple act of taking action and giving it a try.

Being conscientious and proactive and taking responsibility are not things that necessarily come naturally; high-performing people have practised and developed these skills and attitudes over time. These people also recognise that taking bold action involves a higher risk of failure – that's why these actions are considered bold! They overcome their fear, dive in and work out how to swim as they go.

Get on with it!

Try This: When you try something you've never done before, the first minutes and hours are generally tough going, but resist the temptation to give up early. Aim to persevere for at least 15–25 hours. Break that time up into daily or weekly doses of 30 to 60 minutes or even shorter sessions – in fact, anything that will keep you motivated and less likely to give up. Once you've finished the first 15–25 hours, it will be much easier to keep going because you'll have established a new routine.

Start now and commit to measuring your life and its quality based on results, not intentions, because only with results can we be sure that changes are real. Stop accepting excuses from yourself. You move forward in life by establishing new habits and trends, which in turn create their own momentum. Your actions and outcomes then profit from this momentum as you meet new people and new possibilities emerge.

Set goals (see Chapter 7), make a strategy and take action. Develop a sense of urgency about the task you need to perform and get it done. You'll then build momentum that pushes you still further. Waste no more time – get out there and expose yourself to all the great things this world has to offer. There are a lot of opportunities out there just waiting to be discovered.

Remember: Life does not reward your intentions – it rewards your actions. Don't just talk about it: go ahead and pull the trigger!

12

PROCRASTINATION

The biggest roadblock – avoid!

Do you ever procrastinate? I'd be very surprised if you answer no to this question because most of us procrastinate from time to time and 20 per cent of us are chronic procrastinators. Psychologist Piers Steel has discovered that procrastinators perform poorer, feel more miserable, suffer more medical problems and put off important financial decisions such as saving for retirement. Procrastinators don't just delay completing important tasks, they also put off opportunities to enjoy themselves such as waiting too long to book holidays or buy concert tickets.

Why do we procrastinate?

Why put off what needs to be done? Is it just a matter of bad time management, poor willpower or a lack of self-discipline? In fact, it is a little more complicated – there are more deep-seated reasons:

- **Work versus play:** Teachers and parents often believe that schoolchildren procrastinate because of their innate laziness, and to overcome this laziness a child needs reward or punishment or simply to be pushed harder. This understanding of procrastination is too simplistic, however, because before they enter formal education, young children never procrastinate (or rate their performance or care what others think about them). When they arrive at school, they begin to learn subtly that 'work' is no fun and that 'play' is lots of fun, and they begin to learn how to procrastinate. As adults, we mirror this childhood behaviour by creating the same inner conflict. When faced with a task, we say to ourselves 'I *have* to do XYZ' which indirectly means 'I'd rather not do XYZ'. This inner conflict causes tension, stress and a negativity about tasks we categorise as 'work'.

- **Perfectionism:** Many of us suffer from a form of unhealthy perfectionism. If we think anything less than the very best isn't satisfactory, we create unrealistic expectations leading to hesitation about the job in hand.

- **Confusion over what we need to do:** Problems occur when it's not clear what exactly qualifies as a 'good job'. If we're not sure what 'good' looks like or what 'good enough' looks like, we don't know how to live up to others' expectations.

- **A mechanism for coping with stress:** Psychologists have also found that procrastination is caused by a subliminal longing for immediate pleasure. Procrastination provides an instant, though short-lived, respite from the pressures of a busy schedule. Hitting the pause button while we check out a few of our favourite websites or watch TV is one way of lessening the burden for a few minutes or hours.

- **Avoidance of failure:** We all need to be appreciated, valued and held in high regard by others, and we employ many strategies to protect our self-esteem from failures. If a particular task seems too difficult to accomplish, procrastination allows us to reframe the situation. The internal dialogue goes something like this: 'I'm not failing because I'm not able to do it; it's because I haven't attempted to do it.' Procrastinating, then, helps us avoid the worry caused by our fear of failure.

For these reasons, when we're faced with a task that looks boring or stressful or holds an unacceptable risk of failure, we decide that if we don't start work, we can sidestep these outcomes. And procrastination works: it helps us avoid stress, boredom and fear of failure – but only for the moment!

Chronic procrastination

When we constantly avoid getting things done, we're engaging in destructive or 'chronic' procrastination. Chronic procrastination takes you down a path to misery:

1. You delay your work.

2. You build a bigger and bigger mountain of guilt over falling behind.

3. You permanently feel like you have more work to do than you'll ever be able to get done, and you can never truly relax.

Habitual procrastinators rarely enjoy their work – or their life for that matter. Failing to complete tasks and meet goals leaves them stricken with shame and guilt. They're plagued by feelings of failure, which causes stress and anxiety.

The big question is then – how do we kick the habit? All we need is a change of mindset and a few simple tools.

Change your inner dialogue

Firstly, change your attitude to that of a person who doesn't *have* to perform these tasks but really *wants* to perform them. Say to yourself things like:

- I really want to do this.
- I will do this – it's no problem.
- When can I get cracking?

Using this internal dialogue, you, and no one else, will be deciding what needs to be done, when it needs to be done and how best to go about it.

Be willing to make mistakes

Telling ourselves that mistakes are to be avoided at all costs and that failure is intolerable makes us procrastinate. Most high-performing people, on the other hand, don't fear mistakes or setbacks; they just get on with it. And if they do fail, they try to work out why and give it another go.

The vital takeaway here is that if you never try then you'll never learn and you'll never get better. Only those who try and try again are continually refining their skills. Simply put, failure is an expected and accepted part of learning. Therefore, embrace this anti-procrastination mantra: 'Every failure is a learning opportunity.'

Now is the time

We have a tendency to wait for 'the right time', even though that perfect time may never arrive. If this sounds like you, stop waiting for the right time and start taking action now. Why shouldn't this moment be the one you're waiting for?

Get started

Another roadblock that procrastinators often encounter is the simple act of getting started. Instead of actually writing that document, they check their emails, check their phone or chat to colleagues.

Try This: In these situations, I recommend these tools:

- **The ten-minute rule:** Simply start a task with the intention of spending only ten minutes on it. Because you're only committing ten minutes of your time, there's no great hardship, it seems relatively simple and you're more likely to begin. And once you've begun, you've achieved your objective – simply to get started. Who knows how much work you'll do, but at least you've begun, which is an achievement in itself.

- **The five-second rule (designed by Mel Robbins):** When you're at your desk and about to begin a piece of work, simply count down, 'Five, four, three, two, one, GO!' As you utter the word 'GO', start typing, or pick up your phone and make that call. If you're looking for inspiration to begin a physical task, stand up and count down, 'Five, four, three, two, one, GO!' As you utter the word 'GO', start moving in any way, shape or form toward the place where you need to be. This simple act diverts your attention away from fear, excuses or non-productive activities and directs it toward what needs to be done. Do this on every occasion when you'd normally procrastinate – it really does work!

The five-second rule and the ten-minute rule are especially valuable when you can't find the motivation to start. Because procrastination is just another way of rendering yourself powerless, these tools will help you reaffirm proactive control over your day-to-day activities.

Try This: Another way to get started is by persuading yourself that you've already started. Add a few completed items to your to do list and put a line through them. This builds momentum, which encourages you to address the next few items on the list.

Try This: Mornings don't have to mean resentfully dragging yourself out of bed. Plan to start the day with an enjoyable task, which will help incentivise you to get out of bed and begin your day with enthusiasm and energy.

Break down the task

Procrastination is particularly prevalent when a task is so large and overwhelming that the finish line seems far away. This is especially true for big goals, such as gaining a major qualification, learning a language or writing a book. Because there are no rewards or milestones along the way, we easily become demotivated and succumb to the lure of procrastination.

The solution is to divide your work into smaller tasks that are easily completed in relatively short periods of time. If something can be started and finished in an hour or less, it'll be much easier to find the energy to begin. You can experiment with exactly how you decide to divide the task: slices of 15, 30, 60, 90 or 120 minutes – whatever works best for you and your schedule.

When you've completed each slice, you'll feel a tangible sense of achievement, which will motivate you to begin the next slice. This is how you build up the much-needed drive and enthusiasm to keep going and get the job done. You could also boost motivation levels by giving yourself small rewards at key stages along the way.

Set regular deadlines

University students are notorious procrastinators, often waiting until the last minute before doing their work. An experiment with students, however, revealed that they made big improvements when they set themselves small, evenly spaced deadlines throughout their course. This forced them to even out their workload and not procrastinate until the last minute, resulting in far better grades than those of students who had one big deadline at the end of the course. The key takeaway here is to commit to many mini deadlines, which together lead to achieving a major deadline.

In a similar way, yearly targets generally result in a lack of urgency. On the 1st of January, the 31st of December is a long way away, so in the first days and weeks of the year, it's easy to drag our feet a little as there is little tangible deadline pressure at such an early stage.

Try This: Shorter planning periods bring greater urgency, so try the following simple planning protocol:

- **Make a ten-week plan:** Decide what needs to be done and when in the next 10 weeks.

- **Make weekly plans:** Convert the 10-week plan into 10 weekly plans. Each weekly plan should list activities and targets for each day.

- **Weekly assessment:** At the end of each week, make yourself accountable by assessing your progress against your plan. If you fall behind, you'll obviously need to make some adjustments.

Positive accountability

When we're struggling to get everything done, we often make excuses. We say things like 'I'm so busy keeping up with my emails, I have little time for my important project' or 'I'll start running again when my major project is complete'. Excuses like these are sometimes valid, but usually they're just handy comfort blankets to hide under. Don't justify your procrastination with poor excuses. Re-visit your goals, remind yourself of your priorities and make a new plan. And make yourself accountable to that plan by regularly reviewing your progress.

Also watch out for distractions, which vary from others needing your attention to your simply choosing to do other, less important tasks, which is effectively another form of procrastination.

Remember: One of the benefits of having a well-planned anti-procrastination strategy is that it liberates you from an over-reliance on motivation and willpower (see Chapter 13). Your mindset, environment, schedule and accountability should be designed in such a way that they support you during those tough times when energy is low.

13

MOTIVATION, WILLPOWER AND DETERMINATION

The best procrastination busters.

People sometimes think that those who make it in life are the smartest and most talented. This is untrue: success is determined by things that are much more within your control, and prominent among them are motivation, determination and willpower.

Motivation

How do you answer this question: 'What do you do for a living?' You may reply automatically 'I work for an IT company' or 'I work in marketing'. How do you sound as you reply? Do you sound enthusiastic about your job? If the answer is no, it's time for a new approach because finding and appreciating the true purpose and meaning of your work and wider interests will help you feel much more motivated.

Try This: Ask yourself a new question: 'How often and to what extent does my work benefit other people?' Those 'other people' can be any beneficiaries of your work, inside or outside of your company. Say your answer out loud and add as much detail as you can. How do you sound now? Hopefully this little injection of purpose and self-worth will help you feel more enthusiastic and motivated about your job.

Also ask yourself, 'What past difficulties have I had to deal with?' Then ask, 'How did I motivate myself to deal with those difficulties?' You've probably come through some difficult problems in life, so hopefully you can find some positive memories to inspire yourself to handle the challenges of today.

Try This: Each day, stop and ask yourself:

- How can I make a difference today?
- What giant leap forward can I make today?

Willpower

When partaking in fun activities, motivation comes easily. When we need to wash the car or clean out the fridge, however, it's much harder to get motivated. Motivation also depends on our mood – when we feel great, it's easy to go on a short run first thing in the morning, but it's harder if we've had a poor night's sleep and are worrying about that breakfast meeting at work. Motivation levels can also drop when certain repetitive activities get a little tedious.

For these reasons, we cannot rely on motivation alone to build positive habits. Luckily, there's another discipline that we can acquire to pick up the slack when motivation levels are low – *willpower*. And the more we flex our willpower muscle, the stronger it gets.

Willpower, unlike motivation, is dependable and robust. Research from Stanford University has demonstrated that young children with greater than average willpower grew up to achieve greater than average success in their studies, careers and social lives.

If it's so good for us, why don't we demonstrate stronger willpower more regularly? Because we find it easy to postpone unpleasant tasks so that we can indulge ourselves in the present. When an immediate reward is available, any bigger rewards for which we must wait tend to lose their attraction.

Do you think you have strong willpower? Many of us think we do, but often we're deceiving ourselves. The good news is willpower can be strengthened through training and repetition. Every time you create a new positive habit, such as exercising each day, your willpower reinforces itself and becomes stronger.

Sometimes, however, establishing these new habits can be tricky. Imagine, for example, that you have set yourself a goal of getting up early and running for 50 minutes every day before work. Your motivation levels will be high enough to get you up and running for a day or two, but by day three it's possible that your willpower will weaken, and it won't be long before you quit. So how do we intensify our willpower when we most need it – for example, when we're trying to establish a new but challenging habit?

Try This: One idea is to adopt 'mini habits'. Basically, you set small – almost ludicrously small – goals. Our willpower is weakened by perceived hardship of the task ahead, particularly when energy levels are low, so begin by initially choosing an easy target. For example, if you set yourself a goal of getting up early and running for 10 minutes every day before work; this might be a habit that you can more easily maintain. After a few weeks, when the habit is established and has become part of your everyday routine, you might find it relatively easy to run for 15 minutes every day. When you're comfortable with 15 minutes of running, you might consider 20 minutes, then 25 minutes and so on.

By initially picking relatively easy goals, you eliminate perceptions of difficulty and you feel less overwhelmed. Mini habits will get you moving, and once you're in motion, you'll need less willpower to continue. When introducing positive changes to our lives, the greatest barrier we face is the first one: changing from inertia to mobility and mini habits are a great tool to help make this transformation.

Start small, and don't overdo it. Your energy is a valuable commodity and willpower will help you manage it efficiently. Time and energy are not limitless and each day you can only give your attention to a finite number of things, so don't try to change everything in your life at once. Don't over-train your 'willpower muscle'; focus on changing one behaviour at a time.

For more on habits, see Chapter 22.

Determination

Motivation and willpower will give you a solid grounding for success, but they need to be accompanied by determination. Sheer determination will keep you moving forward, whatever obstacles are put in your way.

When we face rejection, for example, we might overdramatise it and conclude that everyone and everything is against us. But remember that many people experience rejection every day. It is not personal; it happens to each and every one of us as we push our boundaries and grow. Therefore, if you can find the determination and resilience to calmly accept rejection or any other roadblock that comes your way, you will enjoy the journey far more.

How many of us have started something new but have given up at the first sign of trouble? Many of us lack the determination we need to achieve our goals, so how do we change this? Determination comes from:

- **Practising hope:** When you believe wholeheartedly that things can change and move in a positive direction, this will dramatically impact your willingness to make those changes happen. When you're hopeful, you feel more empowered to take action.

- **Adopting a critical, wide perspective of any adversity you encounter:** It is normal to feel awful when our deficiencies are exposed, but if we adopt a wider perspective, we'll see that many people, probably the vast majority of people, share similar insecurities. In fact, the power of sheer determination and effort is often harnessed even more by those who have to battle a bit harder – those with a lack of natural talent or experience.

If you're happy with your performance level at any given activity, that's absolutely fine. However, if you want to get any better, you will need a level of determination that enables you to stay persistent when the going gets tough. Whenever you're practising or learning a new skill, ask yourself:

- Am I concentrating fully?
- Am I getting optimum use out of this time?
- What precisely do I need to develop right now?

Remember: Determination is the attitude that keeps you moving forward on those days when everything seems to be against you. It helps you find that extra bit of energy when your tank is empty. In time, determination, motivation and willpower will reap huge rewards.

14

FEAR

What are you afraid of? It's time to challenge your fears.

Thousands of years ago, fear helped people evade perilous situations, such as being attacked by an enemy or a dangerous animal. In this hostile environment, fear was a beneficial approach, alerting people to impending threats and preparing them to either flee or fight. Today, few of us are at risk of being killed by animals or humans, yet we still experience fear on a regular basis. Unfortunately, our modern-day fears are mostly unhelpful. For example, if social fear prevents you from going to a party, the fear isn't beneficial – quite the opposite – it's preventing you from having fun while making some potentially rewarding social connections.

Fear is also drummed into us throughout childhood. When we were young, our well-meaning parents constantly warned us about the risks and hazards of the outside world, teaching us to be on the lookout for potential danger and to do everything possible to remain safe.

Fear is something we all feel, but if we take the time to learn more about our specific fears, we can adopt approaches to minimise them and cope with them.

The big underlying fear

There are many different fears in the world: fear of death, fear of financial ruin, fear of flying, fear of failure, fear of rejection, fear of speaking in public, fear of difficult conversations and the general fear of being vulnerable. Some fears depend on circumstances over which we have little or no control, such as fear of flying. Most fears, however, have little to do with the outside world – they come from within! The majority of fears boil down to one, all-encompassing fear: the fear that we won't be able to handle the difficulties that life throws at us. For instance, fear of being vulnerable and fear of failing stem from the fear of being unable to deal with either scenario should they actually happen.

So let's now ask ourselves this question: would we still be afraid if we believed we could cope with most of life's potential problems? The answer is generally no. We can therefore minimise our fears by having more faith in our ability to cope with these potential problems. With this attitude, we can overcome our fears internally without needing to control the external world. In short, try to adopt this mantra: 'Whatever happens, I'll deal with it.'

It's not as bad as you think

Another key thing to bear in mind is that most of our fears are totally out of proportion with the actual risks involved. For example, a fear of flying is ultimately a fear of death. Yet most people who refuse to set foot on an aeroplane will happily sit in a car for hours and hours even though statistically they're 30 times more likely to die in that car! We might also resist asking someone for a favour for fear of what the other person might think, whereas data demonstrates that the average request receives a constructive and sympathetic reaction three times more than expected. People generally like to help people. Worries about being negatively judged are usually miscalculated, because in reality everyone is too preoccupied with what's going on in their own lives to spend too much time thinking about yours.

Researchers have demonstrated that only 10 per cent of what we worry about actually happens; therefore, 90 per cent of our worries are a complete waste of time and mental energy. Statistically speaking, embracing a more positive outlook is seemingly a better predictor of future events. Also, positive thinking actually inspires us to go out into the world and make our own positive outcomes. Your life will always have challenging situations. Having a positive outlook doesn't involve rejecting the reality of those situations, but it does provide us with the determination to tackle them head on.

Try This: If you consider yourself to be a fearful person, cast your mind back in time to provide a reality check. Complete this sentence: 'I was courageous when I …'. You've most likely done some brave things in your life, and by reliving those moments, you will nurture and progress your bravery still further.

Tools for overcoming fear

The next time you need to face a specific fear:

1. List all of the things that might cause a problem and guestimate the probability of each of those problems actually materialising. You will probably discover that many of your potential problems are either so small or so unlikely that there's nothing to get overly stressed about.

2. Disconnect your emotional wellbeing from the consequences. Try to let go of any speculation around potential negative outcomes. If you simply cannot ignore these potential outcomes, then try not to care so much about them. Minimise their intensity. By removing your emotional wellbeing from the consequences, you reduce tension and feel more calm and composed.

Try This: Another technique you might like to employ is positive visualisation. Visualising yourself doing something that's daunting and new, provides a stepping stone toward coping with any fears. If you run a mental movie of yourself doing something scary, your brain gets more familiar and comfortable with the idea. And more familiarity means less fear.

Prepare to fail – and succeed

How often does fear make you avoid certain situations? Unfortunately this is counterproductive because avoidance serves only to reinforce the fears that hold you back. Suppose you're in a social situation and want to meet someone you're attracted to, but your fear of failure stops you from doing anything about it. The end result is the same as failure, except you haven't even tried. It's a wasted opportunity. Don't allow too many good opportunities to pass you by, or you'll live a life full of regret.

Many people fear that they won't be accepted for who they are, and this fear prevents them from interacting with others. For example, when we see peers whose skills surpass our own, we might feel the urge to simply withdraw from the situation. Comparing yourself with the brightest and the best leads to loss of confidence in your abilities, so try to avoid comparing yourself to other people and just get stuck in and see what happens. We're all on a different journey and we all have different strengths and weaknesses.

Fear of failure is a fear that crops up time and time again and if we're not careful it can stop us before we've even started, so it's vital that we challenge it head on. Trying new things will inevitably result in failure from time to time, but it's a critical part of moving forward, so try embracing failure rather than avoiding it. (Turn to Chapter 26 for more on failure.)

There are no wrong decisions

Another major fear we have is that of making the wrong decisions in life. Rather than agonise over what might happen if we make the wrong choice, adopt the mindset that there are few incorrect decisions, just different ways to experience life. We need to be prepared to take risks and occasionally make some tough decisions. Every new adventure presents new life experiences, knowledge and feedback irrespective of the outcome.

For example, say you finally have a stab at karate after years of thinking about it. If it turns out that you don't particularly enjoy people striking you with their hands and feet, then so be it – but you've made some new friends and learned more about karate. Maybe you find that you'd like to try judo or a similar new hobby. The point is: you need to make the decision to try.

Do something that scares you every day

The more you face fear, the easier it gets. For example, say you're an executive with a disabling fear of public speaking. Yet despite this, you force yourself to give speeches and presentations through sheer grit and determination. After your fifth presentation, you'll be wondering what all the fuss was about!

The more you expose yourself to your fears, the fewer obstacles you'll have that separate you from where you want to be, so make it a regular habit to push yourself beyond your comfort zone. As you address your fears and deal with them, one by one, there will be fewer and fewer fears to slow you down and your confidence will keep on growing. Eventually, they'll be very little that scares you.

Live life to the maximum and be fully committed to everything and anything that is important to you. This will give you a robust, multifaceted foundation, so if one part of your life goes wrong, you will have the other parts to fall back on.

Fear of scarcity

Do you think of yourself as a big-hearted person who gives unconditionally? Or do you normally anticipate something in return? Most of us fall into the second category because we're subconsciously worried about depriving ourselves – we fear scarcity. So how do we overcome this fear and become more generous? Try the following:

- **See how plentiful your life is.** Understand how lucky you are to have so much. Write down everything that you like about your life and every day try to notice and appreciate the positive things that happen – even tiny things like the gentle kind-hearted smile of a passer-by. (For more on gratitude, see Chapter 52.)
- **Make a habit of giving.** Give gratitude and time as well as money and possessions, and witness the magical effect it has on you and the world around you. (For more on generosity, see Chapter 51.)

Push through the fear

We've all come across people who appear to be courageous, confident risk-takers. Here's the thing: these people aren't as fearless or courageous as you think! They've just found a way to recognise and deal with their fear. Fear is a normal and natural part of life that we all experience and we all need to face. Each time we deal positively with our fear we gain the confidence required to take on the next challenge.

Power pose

Social psychologist and Harvard professor Amy Cuddy has performed research that suggests that those people who remain confident and calm in stressful situations had more of the 'dominance' hormone testosterone and less of the 'stress' hormone cortisol in their systems. She also conducted an experiment to discover whether changing body language could alter the levels of these hormones and therefore change the way people feel. Participants were asked to adopt a high-power pose or a low-power pose for two minutes and then asked how confident they felt. They also supplied a saliva sample so that their hormone levels could be measured.

Her results proved that adopting a high-power pose for two minutes did indeed raise testosterone and reduce cortisol levels, leaving participants reporting a stronger sense of confidence and reduced nervousness. Participants adopting a low-power pose reported the opposite feelings along with having lower testosterone and higher cortisol levels in their saliva. Similar experiments conducted in real-life interview situations produced similar results.

Try This: Before you go into any stressful situation, find a private space and go into a high-power pose for two minutes. A high-power pose involves standing tall with a straight, upright posture. Throw your shoulders back, hold your head high and smile. This will hopefully help you tweak your brain chemistry and make you feel a little more confident so you can present the best version of yourself. Good luck!

Remember: Everybody feels fear from time to time, but it's not the fear that's the big issue here; it's how we handle the fear. Every time you move out of your comfort zone you'll feel afraid. So go ahead and let yourself feel afraid and know that it's okay because it means you're asserting yourself and moving forward. In the words of the excellent author Susan Jeffers, 'Feel the fear and do it anyway!'

15

QUESTIONS

Get the right answers: ask the right questions.

If we want to make positive changes to our lives, we must improve the way we think, and essentially, critical thinking can be stripped down to a number of questions and answers. The questions we ask provide a pathway to the answers, so the nature of these questions, therefore, has a huge influence on the direction of our lives.

The power of questions

If a random person stops you in the street and asks if you feel unfulfilled, this is probably not a harmless question. It's the type of seemingly innocuous question a religious street recruiter might use to initiate a conversation. The question plays on our inclination to centre in on what's presented to us, as opposed to the opposite. When someone asks, 'Do you feel unfulfilled?' it encourages us to look for any lack of fulfilment in our lives, not fulfilment. Advertisers and cold-callers also use this psychology to manipulate us by framing their questions in a way that will influence our answers.

Scientists San Bolkan and Peter Andersen conducted an experiment in which researchers asked random people to try out a new soft drink and also give out their email address. Half the test group were initially asked if they were adventurous people who enjoyed trying new things. 76 per cent of this group sampled the drink and provided their email address to the researchers. The other half weren't asked the initial 'are you an adventurous person' question, and amazingly only 33 per cent of this group sampled the drink and provided their email address.

The wrong questions

So how can we use this phenomenon to positively adjust our thinking habits? When something goes wrong, for example, do you tend to say to yourself 'This always happens to me – why?' This is a poor question because it directs your thinking toward what's wrong with your life. It's therefore very important to ask yourself more positive questions.

This isn't always easy, especially in difficult situations. When we're overwhelmed, we often jump to the *wrong* question:

- Why is this happening to me again?
- What's the point in carrying on?
- Why is life so prejudiced against me?

- Why am I not appreciated?

It's very easy to get dispirited by these questions because their negative framework elicits negative responses. Many people also say no instead of yes to things, simply because they pose questions to themselves that promote hesitation:

- What if there's something amazing around the corner?
- If I sign up now, I might miss out on something else in the future?

These questions amplify the fear of missing out on some imaginary scenario and they could stop you from experiencing and appreciating what you can have now.

The right questions

Try This: If you're feeling down, it could be because you're ignoring all the reasons why you should be feeling good, so make a habit of asking questions like these:

- What's good about this?
- How can I enjoy the process of solving this problem?

If you're stuck in the middle of a crisis, these positively framed questions will lift your mood. You'll then be better equipped to arrive at an effective solution or cope with the consequences.

More examples of good questions are as follows:

- How can I make the most of this situation?

- Why am I the lucky person to have you?
- What am I enjoying the most about my life?
- What motivates me?
- What am I proud of?
- What am I grateful for?

Remember: If you ask questions like this, your answers will help you find many reasons for you to feel happy and not unhappy. Companies benefit when they ask the right questions about products and customers, and our personal relationships benefit when we ask the right questions about each other's problems and how we can help each other.

16

DECISIONS

Do you have problems making decisions?

Each and every day we're faced with a multitude of decisions. Some of these are relatively small, such as deciding what shoes to wear or what to have for lunch. Others are big and life changing, such as where to live or what career path to follow. Most of us usually follow sound decision-making strategies, but sometimes we fall prey to a number of misconceptions, biases and our old friend procrastination.

As discussed in Chapter 14, we often fear making the wrong decision. Should I spend lots of money on home improvements or buy a new house? Should I accept that job offer or stay where I am? Negative thinkers view their decisions through a negative lens and worry about making the 'wrong' decision. Of course, we never know what will happen in the future, so there are very few wrong decisions, just different life journeys, and these will probably work out fine one way or another.

Because we tend to follow in the footsteps of those around us (this is called social contagion), try to commit to decisions that are truly your own. For example, you might think you want to play tennis, but in fact you only play tennis because your peers play it. We also follow others when making important decisions regarding careers, house buying and having children: forget what everyone else is doing and just be true to yourself.

Practise by making snap decisions

If you're prone to chronic indecisiveness, try to unlearn this habit by forcing yourself to make snap decisions in low-stake environments. The next time you're at a restaurant and can't decide what to have, give yourself no more than 20 seconds to decide. The time limit forces you to make an instinctive decision – and probably the right decision! Do this often, especially when the stakes are low, such as when shopping for low-priced items. This new habit of quick decision making will help you become more decisive when making all your decisions, including life's big choices.

Make decisions with a calm mind

While strong emotions can often help us make decisions very quickly, they can often diminish our competency for detailed logical thinking. We should therefore endeavour to make big decisions when we're not in a highly emotional state of mind.

Try This: When making an important decision, take a blank sheet of paper and draw a vertical line down the middle. On the left-hand side, make a note of what your heart is saying to you. On the right-hand side, make a note of what your head is saying to you. Now compare the two sides of the paper. What does this tell you? Is your heart ruling your head disproportionately? Or vice versa?

Beware errors of judgement

Because the mind prefers to use the minimum amount of energy possible, it sometimes oversimplifies the situation, leading to errors of judgement. In his excellent book *Thinking, Fast and Slow*, Daniel Kahneman highlights a number of common mistakes we all make. I discuss this in more detail in Chapter 33, but here's a brief overview.

The halo effect

We have a tendency to like or dislike a person or organisation based on very little information. This 'halo effect' is a common bias that plays a large role in shaping our views of people, organisations and situations. In basic terms, if we like or dislike one thing about a person, it follows that we like or dislike everything about them. This is why first impressions are so important.

Confirmation bias

We tend to agree with viewpoints that concur with our opinions. Confirmation bias also leads us to accept and believe information without checking its validity.

Availability bias

This occurs when we overestimate the probability of an event if we've heard about it frequently or recently, or if it's something we find easy to remember, such as anecdotal evidence. We should therefore try to estimate the probability of an outcome based on a credible statistic, not the latest news feed or anecdote.

Overconfidence bias

Everything makes sense with hindsight, right? Problems arise, however, when our interpretation of past events promotes too much confidence in predicting future events. We also tend to have too much confidence in our intuitions. Overconfidence also encourages us to overlook statistical evidence or make oversimplified judgements of complex information.

Overconfidence is particularly prevalent when making financial forecasts. For example, both sellers of company shares and buyers of those same shares, think the market price is incorrect. The buyers think the price is too low and the sellers think it is too high. Both the buyers and the sellers think they know where the price is heading, but obviously only half of them will be correct at any one time.

In the workplace we vastly overrate our capacity for predicting a prospective employee's future success via an orthodox job interview, yet research indicates that relying on a job interview to assess the future performance of an individual is only slightly better than flipping a coin! Also, when projecting the outcomes of new initiatives, managers too often make overconfident predictions rather than thoroughly analysing the available input data. They overestimate future sales and underestimate the costs of materials, staff and a multitude of things that can go wrong. Therefore, whenever it's appropriate, we should replace human judgement or 'intuition' with checklists, procedures and formulae.

Simplify your choices

In 210 BC Chinese commander Xiang Yu sailed his army across the Yangtze River. He then made the bold decision to burn and destroy his own ships, to show his soldiers that retreat was no longer a possibility. This motivated them to fight so intensely that they went on to win battle after battle after battle. As the story illustrates, limiting our choices can be advantageous because it centres our attention on the job at hand.

We often try to keep our options open for as long as we can, but delaying making decisions is often a waste of time and energy. Rather than fooling ourselves that we can keep all doors open indefinitely, at some point we need to make clear decisions about what we really want from life.

Making decisions can be stressful and it doesn't help that our average day is full of both major and micro decisions. It might therefore be a good idea to reduce your daily choices in ways that suit your preferences. For example, could you keep your workday wardrobe simple? Can you stick to a regular menu of meals, to reduce both decision-making and shopping time? Think about all the daily decisions that you make and try to minimise those that waste your time or use up too much mental energy.

Remember: High achievers are clear about their values and goals so making decisions comes easy to them. When you're feeling indecisive, review Chapters 1 (Values), 7 (Goals) and 8 (Priorities) and hopefully you'll find the inspiration to move forward to where you want to be!

17

VULNERABILITY

Turn down the shame dial. Embrace your vulnerability.

We've all experienced shame in one form or another – it is caused by our sensitivity to what others think of us. Humans are social animals and we've evolved to seek social connections with other humans. For many people any form of social disengagement causes mental pain, accompanied by a belief that they're not deserving of individual relationships or of belonging to a group.

Shame emanates from a fear of being criticised or rejected, or of not being good enough. This in turn stops us from trying new things or reaching out, which further disconnects us from others. Shame avoidance discourages us from taking risks at work or with our relationships, or simply trying something different. Shame avoidance is also the most common tool we use to protect our vulnerability. The irony is, however, to escape this vicious circle, we need to actually embrace our vulnerability. And to do that, we must first learn how to free ourselves of shame over who we are and what we've done.

It's good to talk

Shame is an emotion associated with those negative characteristics of ourselves that we think we should conceal. Shame is fear of self-exposure, so it's not something we usually want to talk about for fear of more self-exposure, or in more extreme cases, fear of rejection. Discussing shame also requires us to relive the pain it causes. Because shame gains control through being a secret, the less we speak about it, the more power it has over our lives, so talking about our shame actually diminishes its power.

In general, we will feel better when we discuss our feelings of shame with other people, especially when they offer empathetic and helpful comments in return. Knowing that someone else has been through similar situations or can fully comprehend your situation, will give you the feeling of being understood and you'll feel less alone. Your anxieties soften as you start to feel understood, and you can substitute your negative thoughts of shame with positive thoughts of empathy and compassion for yourself.

Hearing helpful and sympathetic comments from friends is highly therapeutic, but it's also important for you to listen and empathise with them. Try to see things from their viewpoint without passing judgement, which means being sympathetic and engaged with the other person's story.

Recognise your shame

People who identify their shame and what causes it are much better at handling it. For example, our negative body image is a regular source of shame. The media manipulates and amplifies our tendency to worry about how inadequate we are, in an attempt to 'shame' us into buying their products. The more you recognise this manipulation, the more you can push back against it.

We must also be careful not to unjustly seize the moral high ground to conceal our shame, as this will exacerbate the problem. Shame and blame are often linked; we sometimes blame others in order to avoid tackling our own thoughts and feelings of shame. In these situations, we're trying to regain control by wielding dominance and superiority by shifting the blame and shame onto others. Most people will identify the injustice and your reputation will be in tatters, so avoid this behaviour at all costs.

Try This: If you're feeling shame, remain as calm as possible, think about your feelings, label them and describe them. Analyse the situation thoroughly and if necessary reach out to others for a second opinion.

Embrace vulnerability

We live in a world where external displays of strength, achievement and winning are admired, whereas vulnerability is linked to weakness, failure and losing. Very few people consider vulnerability a positive trait because we often associate vulnerability with negative outcomes and with exposing our emotions. The best example of this is falling in love. We might love someone, but what if that someone doesn't love us back? This high-stake risk of rejection makes falling in love the ultimate display of our vulnerability. Falling in love is generally considered to be a good thing to happen to us, so it follows that exposing our vulnerability is also a good thing.

Being vulnerable takes courage because we're taking a risk. But vulnerability is actually the origin of many progressive emotions such as love, joyfulness, empathy and compassion, so embrace it and make it work for you and not against you. If you accept your vulnerability, you'll begin to experience your emotions honestly and without censorship. You'll be more loving, more authentic, more empathic and more compassionate, and this will enable you to connect better with others.

When was the last time you asked someone for advice? Do you ever not ask for advice because it might make you look foolish? Asking for advice simply demonstrates that you're human – you have a gap in your knowledge and need some help. People generally love giving advice, so ask away to your hearts content!

Remember: Accept and embrace that you are who you are. Throughout your life you will make some good decisions and some bad decisions. When you make a mistake, don't beat yourself up, just be open to feedback and try and learn from the experience. When others make mistakes, be gentle on them too and express your opinion in a compassionate way. Being vulnerable simply means you have the capacity to experience emotions and occasionally get things wrong. And don't take yourself so seriously – no one else does!

18

HUMILITY

Be more gracious. Show more humility.

Do you have an insatiable desire to talk about yourself and your achievements? Do you constantly need to be the centre of attention?

If you repeatedly talk about yourself and your achievements, people will resent you and eventually avoid you. Self-absorbed and boastful individuals are normally trying to impress their peers, but it usually has the opposite effect. It might sound counter-intuitive, but you're likely to get more admiration the less you seek it out. People like modest people who don't feel the need to draw attention to themselves and continually try to look good. We prefer people who bond with us through our vulnerability and humility and not through an inflated self-image.

Handling criticism

Do any of the following ring true for you when you face criticism?

- You get highly offended by the slightest criticism.
- You get irritated or angry with the individual who's being critical.
- You feel under attack.
- You feel the need to defend yourself whatever the circumstances.
- You retaliate with criticism.

All these overreactions expend a huge amount of mental energy and angst.

In its simplest form, criticism is simply an alternative viewpoint of our actions. If that viewpoint doesn't correlate with the image we have of ourselves, our ego kicks in and we defend or attack. If, however, we're more humble and more open to criticism, we will become less concerned about gaining validation from other people. Simply put, our humility will unlock the door to inner freedom.

Try This: In future, when you get unflattering feedback, try to welcome it and avoid the knee-jerk impulse to tell yourself that the person is wrong. You might even take this strategy one step further and initially agree with the negative comments. This will placate the other person's desire to state their opinion and reduce the chances of a heated argument. Look upon criticism as an opportunity to learn more about yourself or the situation you're in.

Take responsibility

Make sure that you take responsibility for all your actions, and understand that this includes acknowledging where you went wrong. When it's appropriate, offer an apology that isn't fudged with defensiveness or long-winded explanations and excuses. The only way to receive genuine forgiveness, maintain maximum integrity and gain the trust of others is to sincerely accept the blame. If you can then investigate what went wrong and how to improve things, you'll become a much better person.

Connecting to our inner circle through humility

Some of us are unwilling to seek advice from our inner circle of close friends and family. This might be due to us having a sense of superiority or we might feel awkward, or we simply don't expect any of them to have the answers. There could be a lost opportunity here for two reasons:

- The individuals who care about you are in the front seats. They know you so well, that they are in the prime position to come up with suggestions and ideas that you've overlooked.

- This will deepen and strengthen your close relationships because the person you're asking will feel needed, valued and special.

Remember: Acting with humility means focusing on others rather than just yourself and appreciating the value of all things. It means being honest about your shortcomings and being open to self-improvement. When you have a willingness to see yourself truthfully, you will formulate an accurate awareness of your place in the world, and you will be less worried, fearful and insecure.

19

KINDNESS AND COMPASSION

Do you care about others? Then show a little kindness and compassion.

Research shows that people who are kind and compassionate are more satisfied with their lives, have better physical and mental health, and have stronger relationships. Being kind and compassionate helps other people, and it makes you feel good too.

Compassion

Compassion is the process of seeing life from someone else's standpoint and understanding their difficulties and their pain. By being compassionate toward others we change our perspective on life; we open our hearts and offer help and support. Being compassionate boosts our own happiness because we're reminded that we aren't alone and that everyone around us battles with the same problems that we face. And most of us feel a sense of positive karma when helping others.

Self-compassion involves taking a compassionate view of ourselves. If a good friend has something bad going on in their life, would you judge them negatively? Probably not. You most likely would try to help them, right? So why not offer yourself the same patience and compassion that you would offer your friend? Studies demonstrate that self-compassion helps build our resilience because it lessens our propensity to chastise ourselves, which indirectly boosts our self-esteem.

Kindness

Kindness means a lot of things: smiling at strangers, behaving politely, being patient, and being helpful. You might help an elderly neighbour, contribute to a charity, help out at your local school or undertake voluntary work.

The best reason for practising kindness is that it brings pleasure and happiness to your life, rather than serving as a mere tool to seek approval from your peers. Hopefully, you find a few simple acts of kindness to be rewarding because they bring you a step closer to some of the most important qualities in life: helpfulness, compassion and love.

If you're kind enough to do someone a favour, do you expect a favour in return? When we tally up our good deeds in this way, it can diminish the serene feeling that our act of kindness has created within. Because it comes from the heart, an act of kindness should be rewarding and peaceful in its own right, with no worrying about who owes who what. Most of the time we don't need something in return; just a 'thank you' will often suffice. It's tough to be happy if we're filling our mind with comparisons of who does more and who does less, especially at home. If something needs doing, we're often best served by just doing it, instead of fussing over whose turn it is. We'll be happy that we've done our bit and it's one less thing for someone else to do.

Little deeds of kindness

We want to be heard and taken seriously; we want our opinions and ideas to be valued and understood. It's only fair then, that we hear other people and value their perspective. By attempting to 'get' people on a deeper level, you gain an understanding and awareness of their personal journey.

Kind and compassionate people who genuinely listen without judgement are the most trusted, loved and appreciated amongst us. Before sharing your opinion during a conversation, ask yourself if you've really listened. If you don't understand what it would be like to be in the person's shoes, try asking more questions. Simply by taking the time and patience to listen, we radiate compassion and love.

To be more accepting of others, be mindful that we all have faults. We all get jealous, irritated, confused, angry, and so the list goes on. When someone is behaving strangely, try not to overreact – take a step back, pause for a second and try to see the motivation behind that behaviour. What is happening in their lives that's making them behave like this? This change in perspective will help you move from a state of anger to a state of compassion. You'll become less angry and the other person will feel understood – a true win-win situation.

Remember: Mother Teresa once said, 'Not all of us can do great things, but we can all do small things with great love.' She was right. If we can all offer little deeds of kindness to the world, we'll feel the pleasure and joy of helping and we'll make the world just a little bit better.

20

TIME MANAGEMENT

Where does all that time go? Be a better time manager.

How we spend our lives is determined by how we spend our days, which is determined by how we spend our hours and minutes. A daily plan needs to be part of a weekly plan, which is part of a monthly plan, which is part of a yearly plan, which is part of a five-year plan, which is part of a life plan.

Good time managers organise their schedule each day and spend most of it doing things that are important to them. Poor time managers do the opposite and don't spend anywhere near enough time on what is important. We're all guilty of poor time management sometimes, but there's plenty we can do to make better use of our time.

Minimise distractions

Much of our time is spent simply reacting to the relentless flood of information and demands from others. Sending messages and distributing information is now so easy, and the resulting onslaught of messages from email, SMS, WhatsApp, Facebook, Instagram, Twitter, etc. takes up far too much of our time and energy. We're not actively driving our lives forward; we're simply reacting to every trivial thing that comes our way.

A research firm recently reported that 30% of work hours are wasted on disruptions and distractions. We're flooded with huge amounts of new information and we don't know if it's important until we focus our attention on it. For example, if your computer sends an alert to signify a new message, you don't know whether it's SPAM or something interesting until you read it. This, along with other distractions like the pull to check the news or a social media feed, means we're repeatedly side-tracked, and find it difficult to concentrate on important tasks for long enough to complete them.

Furthermore, a continuous inflow of new information and new work can mean that we think we're being productive when we're not. Attending every meeting and conference call, and reading and responding to every email may make you feel like you're working hard, but it says nothing about your ability to complete important projects and make a real difference.

We must, therefore, remove – or at least significantly reduce – all the distractions that interrupt our concentration. Chapter 21 is dedicated to email and electronic devices generally, but for the time being, simply turn off all the alerts for your incoming messages and check your emails and other messages just four times a day. Arrange your workspace to minimise the possibility of interruptions from other people and use your phone's voicemail facility as often as possible.

Try This: If you're enticed by a distraction, try to catch yourself before you shift your attention to it. Take a few slow and deliberate breaths and redirect yourself back to the task at hand. As well as being more productive, those people who minimise distractions are actually happier. In a study at Harvard University, people were found to be more contented when fully immersed in a single activity.

A task and scheduling system

Now we've removed many of the usual distractions, we can get down to business.

Try This: Write down all your goals, projects, tasks and ideas in a master list. Include all the things you're already committed to, such as current duties and projects. This will help you assess how much time you're already using and therefore how much time is left over for your new projects. Decide which items on your list are the most important with respect to your career and personal goals. Be careful not to take on too many things at once – if something can be delegated or dropped completely this is a good time to do it. Break large and complex projects down into smaller actionable tasks.

Now organise your task list into four sub-lists:

- List 1: important urgent tasks
- List 2: important non-urgent tasks
- List 3: unimportant urgent tasks
- List 4: unimportant non-urgent tasks

Generally, the items on List 1 need to be done first, but most of us tend to do our best work when selecting items from List 2. This is where we truly think, where we create, where we innovate and add real value, instead of merely responding to anything and everything that is thrown at us. We might feel industrious when we're working on List 3, but usually that's not true because urgent work is often not high-quality work. List 4 will probably consist of tasks that we can quite easily consider low priority, many of which we can drop altogether.

When checking through your four lists at the beginning of each day, the following two questions will be helpful in deciding on exactly what to prioritise:

- What is my 'must do' task for the day?

- What task will make me feel the most contented and fulfilled at the end of the day?

Develop a paper or electronic scheduling system to organise everything you need to do and when. Be sure to add specific blocks of time in your calendar to complete important work from List 2. Because they're not urgent, these blocks of time are all too easily cancelled for other activities, so try to be disciplined; avoid procrastination, be accountable to your schedule and get the work done.

MIIs

Unless you're definitely not a morning person, address your Most Important Items (MIIs) first, before tackling other tasks. If you complete your MIIs at the beginning of the day, the feel-good factor will create some great momentum for the rest of the day. If you're at your best in the afternoon or evening, adjust your schedule accordingly. If you're not sure, just keep trying different things until your best working patterns become clear.

Keep up to date

Update your lists, your calendar, your filing system and your workspace regularly. This ensures you're not overwhelmed and keeps everything current. Regularly review and remove tasks that are out of date or no longer relevant.

Don't overload yourself or multitask

When making your plans, don't set too many excessively ambitious targets or fill your to-do lists with far too many items. When you do many things at once, you're far less effective, so focus on one task at a time. Multitasking leads to more mistakes, more stress and intellectual exhaustion. Focus and concentration are your most essential and important tools.

Say no more often

If you think about it, every time you say yes to something, you're saying no to something else. Researchers have also discovered that people who are comfortable saying no to non-essential requests for their time enjoy life much more because they have:

- More time: you make more time and space for the people and activities that add value to your life.
- More energy: saying no to a request that saps your energy frees you up emotionally to invest in activities you enjoy.
- More happiness: you feel comfortable knowing that you are living according to your priorities.

Strip out unnecessary meetings or keep them short

Avoid meetings and conference calls where your presence is not essential. You could do this on a trial basis at first – if a specific meeting runs smoothly without you, then you can selectively or regularly miss future meetings.

If your presence at a meeting is essential, don't waste time. Each meeting you attend should:

- Have a clearly stated purpose and outcome.
- Have a time limit.
- Be conducted while standing up. Researchers have found that 'standing' meetings encourage better teamwork, create more solutions and are shorter than 'sitting' meetings.

Delegate

Always be on the lookout for tasks that you can delegate (with clear instructions!)

High-fliers don't need to fully understand something to be able to use it – they're time misers. They focus on key issues and don't waste time on unimportant details. They don't spend time investigating complex issues when they can consult a specialist to answer questions and offer professional advice.

Also, unless you enjoy them, try not to allow basic chores to eat into valuable time. If you can afford it, pay someone else to clean your home or look after your garden.

Conduct a pre-mortem

A great idea to avoid over-optimistic planning is to do a 'pre-mortem'. A pre-mortem is a forward-looking process, rather than a backward-looking process of a post-mortem, the purpose being to identify weaknesses in your forward planning. Imagine it's one year from now and you've failed to achieve one of your goals. Now write down all the reasons that could have caused this to happen.

The main advantage of the pre-mortem is to encourage you to identify potential problems that you hadn't previously considered. This technique is particularly useful for new business initiatives. It overcomes 'groupthink' and enables team members to voice their doubts through a formal process. This will help when discouragement of doubt has created overconfidence in a group.

Have fun

We're often so focused on just getting things done, that we forget about relaxation, relationships, hobbies, sports, health and well-being. We persuade ourselves that when everything is done, we'll be peaceful, stress-free and ready to be happy. Unfortunately, this rarely happens because our 'to-do' list is constantly being refilled with new things to do and we never truly relax.

What we often don't realise is that virtually everything can wait because few things are truly urgent. Each day take a moment to acknowledge that you are not put on this earth simply to tick off everything on your 'to-do' list, but to enjoy the journey and live a life full of joy.

Remember: Sometimes you just need to stop, relax and do something for your own fun and enjoyment, whether it is watching TV, reading or getting outdoors. Try to do what you love as much as possible – there are only so many tomorrows.

21

DEVICES

Do you enjoy new technology? Does it make you happier?

Smart phones, tablets and other devices have become such powerful and versatile tools, they're virtually indispensable. The advantages of this technology are obvious, but what about the disadvantages? I'll begin this chapter by looking into a few of the more common problems, before guiding you through a number of ways to regain control of both your devices and your time.

The dangers of devices

Addiction

Consider these probing questions:

- Do you often spend more time on your devices than you originally planned?
- Do you interact more with people via a screen than in person?

- Do you often interrupt what you're doing so you can check your phone?

If your answers to these questions are mainly yes, then you are exhibiting addictive tendencies toward your phone. When you leave your phone at home deliberately or accidentally, how do you feel? Do you feel nervous? How often do you stop to check your inboxes? Take an average day and log each time you check your inboxes – you may be more obsessed than you think! Compare yourself with the following 2020 survey results from slicktext.com:

- The average time spent on a smartphone is 2 hours and 51 minutes per day.
- Nearly 70% of people check their smartphone within 5 minutes of waking up.
- The average smartphone user checks their phone 63 times per day.
- 46% of parents surveyed said they 'feel addicted' to their smartphones.
- 47% of parents surveyed think their child had a smartphone addiction.

Electronic messaging is highly addictive, and just like any other form of addiction, it can cause behavioural issues. Dopamine is a neurotransmitter which generally make us feel good, and compulsive device checking causes our dopamine levels to increase. It makes us feel aroused, motivated and happy, so we start to crave it. Every unopened message is a curiosity – a potential source of good or exciting news, or an amusing joke, and we crave the spark of delight that each message might give us.

Pressure to reciprocate

Another big issue with electronic messaging is that when we receive a message, we often feel obliged to reply. And because everyone carries their phone around all day and night, we're regularly expected to reply instantly. Messages, information and tasks sent to our phones and laptops continually interrupt our day, generating an endless to-do list. On occasion we feel overwhelmed by all the content coming our way, and frustrated and guilty about the pressure we feel to reciprocate.

Reduced Productivity

When you open and reply to every message the instant it appears, you might feel productive, but often you're achieving very little. Reducing the number of outstanding messages to zero is an enticing reward, but many messages are unimportant and have no impact on your long-term goals. There are usually more vital or significant tasks and activities you could or should be doing with your precious time.

Pulling us away from what really matters

According to data collected in 2019, 86% of all smartphone users will check their devices while in conversation with friends and family and 56% of teens admit to spending large amounts of time in silence, on their phones, while hanging out with friends. Our devices have become a major part of our lives and are clearly changing the way we interact with our families and friends. There are only a finite number of hours in the day, so the more time we spend looking at our phones, the less time we spend with anyone we care about.

Self-editing

When we share information online, we're mindful of how our audience will judge what we say or post. But are we always wholly truthful or authentic? Do we always share the full story, or do we edit – do we, in a sense, perform?

It's possible to hide behind social media and doing so affects our social skills and real connections with people. Social media makes it possible to connect to others in ways that shield us from exposing our vulnerability through our body language or tone of voice. With social media we can take the time to write something or post something that makes the impression we want. Some young people don't like talking on the phone because they have little opportunity to self-edit, and many people avoid real-time conversations by responding to a telephone call with an email or text.

The fallacy of multitasking

Do you ever use your devices while doing something else? Multitasking with devices can trick you into believing that you're being exceptionally resourceful. Research shows, however, that the human brain can only concentrate on one thing at a time, and when it's required to constantly interchange from one thing to another, and back again, it becomes fatigued and poorly functioning.

Over-reliance

Relying too much on our devices can make us less smart and less analytical. Technology has an increasing role in the modern world, but as we transfer significant parts of our intelligence, memory and analytical skills to our phones and computers, the motivation to improve our own minds will diminish.

Take control

To fix many of these problems, we need to take control of when we're reading and responding to messages. Think carefully about which messages are high priority and which are not. How can you reduce or eliminate the time-wasters?

Try to dedicate the first 90 to 150 minutes of your day to important work. For most people, the first few hours of the morning are when the mind is rested and full of energy, so try not to misuse that dynamism on simple or unimportant tasks and emails.

Research suggests that you'll be more productive and less stressed if you deal with emails and other messages at fixed times rather than constantly checking your inbox and responding. Switch off all your audio message alerts and only attend to emails and other messages when you're ready to. It might be useful to let key people at work or at home know that this is your preferred messaging etiquette and if something is urgent, they will need to call you. Avoid checking your devices first thing in the morning or just before bedtime. This will help keep you grounded and in a relaxed mood at two key periods of the day.

Here are a few more tips for managing your emails:

- Delete all irrelevant messages immediately.
- Set up different inbox folders with varying levels of priority, so emails from your boss and other important stakeholders are directed to a folder marked 'urgent' and emails from other contacts go into other folders that vary in terms of importance and priority.
- Don't use your inbox as a to-do list. Your to-do list is yours and yours only, so don't let messages from other people create that list for you. Once you've seen and understood a message,

remove it from your inbox. If a message requires a response, attend to it straightaway or add it to one of your to-do lists, and then file it in an appropriate message or email folder.

- If an email necessitates an extensive response, it's good practice to acknowledge receipt of it immediately and let the other person know when they can expect a full and considered reply.

Keep in mind that phone calls and meetings are usually better than email if you're discussing something important, sensitive or complex. Group emails particularly, can become never-ending and confusing, and key details can get lost.

Quality social interactions

Electronic messaging and video chat platforms are poor substitutes for face-to-face communication. Studies show that real-life interactions facilitate a more coherent link between our words, our body language and our emotions. We empathise more and form stronger emotional and social bonds with our conversation partners. Video platforms such as Zoom, Skype and FaceTime also encourage many people to multitask, which devalues the conversation even more.

Imagine you're sitting with a friend for a coffee and a catch-up, and while you're talking, your friend picks up his phone to read a message. How would you feel? Most people would feel a little put out. Some people would consider it quite rude. Researchers have demonstrated that simply having a phone on the table when chatting with someone diminishes the importance of the conversation, because if we are aware that we might need to attend to a message on our phone, we subconsciously engage in small talk and superficial matters rather than deep and meaningful themes and issues in our lives.

The need for solitude

Solitude and contemplation are important for our mental health and too many distractions from our devices can deprive us of this valuable 'me time'. Psychologists believe that undistracted solitude enables us to access our most insightful thoughts and emotions. Undistracted solitude triggers the section of our mind responsible for profound understanding and wisdom, which in turn helps create a stronger awareness of who we are. Psychologists also believe that solitude improves imagination and innovation – it leaves our minds free to conceive and formulate new ideas.

Set an example and boundaries for kids

Those born since 1996 have been raised with mobile phones in and around their everyday lives and they spend many hours a day on these devices. Researchers point out a worrying rise in psychological health issues in this age group, with high levels of anxiety being top of the list.

Children learn vocabulary, speech styles and associated facial expressions from their parents, so if parent/child interactions are reduced, children have less opportunity to learn the basic social skills they'll need when they're older. When children are regularly disregarded by their primary caregivers due to overuse of devices or other distractions, they begin to disregard other people themselves.

Parents should therefore lead by example and get off their phones, especially in front of those sulky adolescents who seem to do nothing but stare at their phones all day. A few family rules, such as 'no phones at the table', will also reap benefits in the long term. (For more on parenting, see Chapter 55.)

The app audit

According to the Law of Diminishing Returns, we can't just keep adding new apps to our phones and expect to have time for them all. If you decide to remove some of your apps, be clear with yourself as to why you're doing it:

- What is your motivation to remove an app?
- What is your motivation to keep an app?
- Does the app waste your time or save you time?

By asking yourself these questions, you'll ensure that you only keep those apps that really add value to your life.

Remember: Disconnecting from devices and taking some time to reconnect with yourself and be present in the activities taking place around you can be incredibly valuable. There are many apps and other tools to help you monitor and set time limits on your device usage, so give some of them a try. These, combined with a few other lifestyle changes, will help you become less of a slave to your devices and create a healthier and happier lifestyle.

22

HABITS

We are what we do most – do your habits help you or hinder you?

Studies show that regular habits take up about 45 per cent of our time, but why is this? Representing only 2 per cent of the weight of an adult, the brain consumes 20 per cent of the energy produced by the body so it is always looking for ways to conserve energy. We love habits because they enable the brain to function on autopilot and consume less energy.

Most habits consist of three phases:

- The first phase begins with an *external signal* – for example, your morning alarm goes off.
- An appropriate *habitual routine* follows. In this case, you go into the bathroom and do what you do every day without really thinking about it.
- Finally, you get a *reward*, which in this example is being clean, well-groomed and ready to get dressed.

Your brain then recognises a successful completion of the routine, reinforcing the connection between the external signal, the habitual routine and the reward. Reinforcing the connection in this way gives the habit a measure of resilience.

Habit resilience can be a good or a bad thing. An addictive smoking habit with a strong measure of resilience means that if we succeed in giving up for a period, we'll continually be in danger of lapsing. On the positive side, if a good habit such as exercising is resilient, this will work to our advantage.

Craving

When a habit such as taking drugs, smoking or eating chocolate includes an element of 'craving', then its level of resilience hits the stratosphere. Healthy habits, such as exercise, can also benefit from an element of craving, whether it is a craving for an endorphin 'high' or a reward such as a personal best. With many habits, people look forward to the reward so much that denying it will make them irritated and moody. This is the essence of craving.

If you ask any smoker, they'll tell you that it's very hard to weaken their craving for nicotine. One strategy for giving up is to acknowledge the craving but react to it with something different to smoking. In other words, don't fight the craving, just find a different habitual routine and reward.

Alcoholics Anonymous (AA) use this method to great effect. They are one of the most successful habit-changing groups on the planet, helping thousands of alcoholics stay sober every year. When asked what they need or crave from alcohol, AA members often cite things like relaxation and companionship and not necessarily inebriation itself. AA will then suggest new habitual routines that satisfy these cravings, such as attending meetings and chatting to other members for comradeship and establishing new, alcohol-free friendships.

Core habits

Good core habits that create positive outcomes give us the confidence to change habits in other areas of our lives. For example, medical professionals often find it difficult to get highly overweight individuals to make wide-ranging improvements to their routine. However, when these people are asked to focus on developing one core habit, such as taking a 10-minute walk each day, other good habits begin to follow.

A core habit works best if it provides small and quick wins, which provide the positive feedback and momentum required to help start more good habits. High performers deliberately and meticulously adopt core habits that work for them, and once established they make it a priority to practise these habits come what may.

Breaking a habit

So how do you break a bad habit? Begin by being more mindful and aware of what you're doing when you indulge in the bad habit. Look for the external signals as they occur and try to stop and think before you feed the habit yet again. This is self-control in action, and like any other personal skill, self-control strengthens through practice and repetition. We do tend to overestimate our ability to control ourselves and some habits are hard to break, so expect a few slip-ups along the way. Try to learn from each setback; come up with some ideas and then make plans to avoid lapsing in the future.

If you want to stop smoking, the simple act of just trying to stop for a short period will be a good start. For example, once you know you can go without a cigarette for one hour, you can try going for two hours. When you can stop for one day, you can try going for two days, and so on.

You could also try to substitute your bad habit with a better one. For example, replace that cigarette with chewing gum or replace that huge piece of cake with something healthier. Don't try to resist the craving, just acknowledge it and redirect it by experimenting with different substitutes.

Establishing a new habit

Before you begin a new habit, make sure you know exactly why you want to start. Thoroughly analysing your motivations and goals in this way will help you identify and overcome any barriers that are likely to halt your progress. If your new habit is to run outside every day, your barriers are likely to be tough weather conditions and bodily aches and pains. Plan for these obstacles by posing some 'If A, then B' problems and solutions. For example, 'If the weather is awful, then I will wear warm or wet-weather clothes on my morning run.'

To keep motivated, you might need to introduce a degree of variety. This might mean using different routes for your morning run, or it might mean intentionally stopping to listen to the birds or admire a view, or to stroke the dog of a passer-by.

Hopefully, you can now create a habit simply by repeating the activity, and over time it will get easier and easier. But if you're struggling to adopt the new habit and you're desperate to make it stick, try these strategies:

- **Set a much smaller target – a mini habit.** You'll be less overwhelmed, and once you get going, you can build from there. Say you want to learn Italian, why not begin by learning one word each day? Mini habits like this are so small that you'll feel little or no resistance to completing the task. Consistency is the key to creating habits, and by developing your habits slowly but surely, you're most likely to achieve consistency.

- **Make a clear plan.** When embarking on new habits, many of us make ambiguous statements such as 'I'm going to exercise more' without thinking about how or when it will happen. Our chances of success improve if we implement a clearly defined timetable of how, when and where we'll exercise more.

- **Track your progress.** On your timetable, tick off every day that you stay on track. The ticks will enhance the feel-good factor of achievement and encourage you to keep going.

- **Draw up a performance contract.** In this contract, include undesirable penalties if you miss a predefined target. For example, if you fail to hit your exercise targets, you could impose a financial penalty on yourself, maybe as a charitable donation. The donations should be clearly defined in a written contract signed by you and a friend or personal coach. This strategy motivates us by appealing to both our financial and social needs. Because we care what other people think, having someone observe our progress will drive us on to do better.

Remember: We become what we do the most, so establish and maintain the habits you want and ditch the habits you don't want.

23

DIETING

What is your relationship with food?

Many people use eating as a coping mechanism to deal with such feelings as stress, anxiety or boredom, or even to prolong feelings of joy. Unfortunately, this strategy often leads to guilt, which causes even more stress, thus perpetuating a vicious circle of unhealthy overeating. By learning how to make healthier and more mindful choices, you may be able to control compulsive eating, binging and weight gain. If you consider yourself overweight and you'd like to diet, this chapter might help you with some advice on the psychology and physiology of dieting.

Note: It's beyond the scope of this book to guide you on what to eat and when to eat. There are many other sources of information available written by experts with the appropriate qualifications in nutrition, so please do some research if you're unsure.

Small, incremental changes

If you've ever attempted a new diet and then slipped into your previous eating habits a few days later, you're certainly not alone. That's because most new diets require major and sudden changes to your eating habits and lifestyle, and as a consequence, they have a high probability of failure. The key is to adopt small changes at first and slowly build from there. Each small change will build on the previous small change and will accumulate to a much bigger change over a longer time frame. (This strategy draws on the principal of adopting mini habits, as discussed in Chapter 22.)

Try This: Isolate one thing you can do every day to help you eat or drink 50 less calories for that day. Cutting 50 calories out isn't drastic for most people, but if it is too much, try lower, or if it's too easy, try higher. You'll need to find out how many calories are in the various foods and drinks that you consume, but keeping a calorie consumption log is a great idea anyway. There are a few apps available that can help you with this. The target is simply to cut out 50 calories every day, but even if you miss the odd day, don't be discouraged, just try again the following day.

Diets often fail because they're either too drastic or too specific and you end up having to eliminate too many of those treats that you love. This can be very demotivating, so instead, look at your food consumption log and consider how you can eliminate some of the foods that cause you to put on weight, while retaining many of the things you enjoy. A popular approach is to give yourself a specific reward when you've hit a specific target. For example, if you have a healthy lunch or dinner, allow yourself one of your favourite treats that evening. Psychologically this is much more palatable than denying yourself certain pleasures entirely.

Making small changes will reduce the probability of failure and keep you moving in the right direction.

Less is more

One common technique used for dieting is to simply use a smaller plate. Because the plate looks full, our brain is fooled into thinking we've consumed a larger amount of food. The brain then fools our stomach into thinking it's fuller. Conversely, the same portion on a very large plate will leave the eye, stomach and brain hungry for more.

A variation on this theme is to add plenty of low-calorie but 'big' foods to your meal, such as vegetables or salad. This makes the meal visually big enough to satisfy you, while consuming a lower number of calories.

This optical illusion can, however, work against you if your food shelves are filled with huge, oversized packages. They may save money, but when we serve from a jumbo-sized package, we tend to use a larger amount, which in turn means we'll probably eat a larger amount. So try to buy food in smaller packaging, or if you're on a budget, buy jumbo-sized packages and then transfer the contents into smaller containers for day-to-day use at home. Also, oversized bags of crisps and snacks encourage ridiculous amounts of consumption, particularly if you're distracted by a TV or computer. It's therefore a good policy to serve snacks in a small bowl and to stop eating when the bowl is empty.

Mindful eating

It takes around 20 minutes from the time you begin eating for your brain to send out indicators of fullness. Eating slowly is evidently a good thing, but the average person in the USA, for example, consumes lunch in just over 10 minutes. When we eat this quickly, we're more likely to overeat, as our stomach never gets the opportunity to tell us it's full.

Try This: Try to pace yourself and eat very slowly. Put down your knife and fork after every mouthful and chew your food more slowly and deliberately.

Try This: You could also try mindful eating, which involves focussing all your attention on your food for a few minutes. Begin with a single grape, a small berry or a nut. Put it in your mouth and keep it there for a few moments just feeling the contours and texture of the outer surface. When you start to chew, go very slowly. Concentrate on the taste and physical sensations in your mouth as you bite into it. You'll be amazed at the variety of sensory feedback you receive when you eat in this way.

Environmental signals

We often unconsciously follow social and environmental signals to decide when to stop eating. When we eat with other people, we have a tendency to carry on eating until the last person has finished, so quick eaters are more likely to refill their plates and keep eating until the last person stops eating. Too combat this tendency, try to be the last to start eating and then eat slowly. Try matching your pace with the slowest eater at the table.

Also watch out for situations where you're eating while doing something else, such as socialising. At some social events food is served ad hoc in the form of canapés or over many small courses. In the absence of the usual visual cues, it's very difficult to keep track of how much we eat, so we often eat too much. In these situations, try to make a mental note of how much you've consumed, or you'll end up eating until the food stops coming!

Remember: A healthy diet will help to prevent certain long-term diseases such as heart disease, stroke and diabetes. It may also reduce your risk of getting certain cancers and help you to keep a heathy weight. By making better food choices and adopting better eating habits, you will also experience elevated levels of calmness, focus and energy.

24

ALCOHOL

Do you need to drink less?

Consumed in moderation, alcohol isn't necessarily a problem and it can be a pleasant component of a happy and healthy lifestyle. Heavy drinking, however, is bad news. These are just some of the dangers:

- Damages most of the tissues and organs in the body
- Impairs the immune system
- Increases the chances of developing liver, heart, gastrointestinal and upper digestive tract diseases
- Increase the chances of a heart attack, hypertension, a stroke, and cancer of the mouth, throat, oesophagus, larynx, colon and rectum

Depending on which country you live in, 25–40 per cent of admissions to hospital are associated with alcohol in one form or another.

Why drink too much?

High alcohol consumption can be influenced by our genetic make-up, but more often than not it's influenced by the company we keep. If we mix socially with high alcohol consumers, there's a good chance we'll become high alcohol consumers ourselves, because the group 'normalises' everyone's drinking behaviour.

Sometimes drinking extends beyond a social habit to a craving and this is where addiction begins. The body develops a physical addiction that's both subtle and potent. Alcohol raises the levels of two key neurotransmitters: dopamine and serotonin, both of which make us feel good. The brain then identifies surplus dopamine and serotonin and tries to restore equilibrium by decreasing their production, which is why we revert to a lower mood when sober – which in turn causes us to compensate by having another drink. The brain has now become chemically addicted to alcohol.

Other, seemingly innocent triggers for our drinking are boredom, tension, stress and fatigue. A 'pick me up' at the end of a hard day delivers a timely boost to a tired body and weary mind. Unfortunately, alcohol is a depressant and not a stimulant, so the more we drink to fuel our energy levels, the more we need to combat the depressant effect. And the cycle repeats.

Try This: Do you know why you crave alcohol? If you're not sure, begin by keeping a craving log in which you write down the reason for every drink you consume. Keeping track of your 'drinking desire' in this way will make you more aware of why you drink.

After a month or so, look back through your craving log searching for patterns:

- Is alcohol your counsellor?
- Do you drink to mask negative feelings or alleviate boredom?
- Do you drink to raise energy levels, heighten positive feelings or to celebrate?
- Do you drink because everyone else is drinking?
- Do you drink to get drunk?

Now examine the issues behind these motivations. Here are a few classic examples:

- **Drinking for energy:** If a fall in your blood sugar level causes craving, try eating instead. If you often drink due to tiredness, try to work out why you get so tired and make a few adjustments. A good diet, exercise and plenty of sleep are common solutions that will almost certainly reduce your craving for alcohol.

- **Drinking to be sociable:** If people drinking in your company stimulate a craving for alcohol, try reframing your thoughts. It might be daunting at first but think of socialising without alcohol as an adventure – an opportunity for personal growth. Socialising doesn't automatically necessitate alcohol, so rather than consuming alcohol try an alternative drink and find a way to enjoy the company of the people around you.

- **Drinking with the wrong people:** If drinking is a prerequisite to be accepted by a social group, you might want to re-evaluate exactly why you want to hang out with that group. Try to limit the time you spend with people who persistently encourage you to drink too much.

- **Drinking to curb boredom:** If you feel the urge to drink through sheer boredom, set a 15-minute timer on your phone before pouring a drink. Then go and do something else to occupy your mind. When the timer goes off, your craving might have subsided as you're no longer bored. Carry on with what you're doing or set another timer if the craving is still with you. The key takeaway here is to try to engage in more activities where you don't feel the need for alcohol.

If you do fancy a night out with a few drinks, plan the amount that you intend to drink beforehand. Try alternating alcoholic drinks with non-alcoholic drinks, which will have the added benefit of keeping you hydrated. Consume less than one alcoholic drink per hour; your liver breaks down alcohol at the rate of about one unit per hour, so spreading out your drinking in this way lessens the likelihood of a hangover. Also, be selective with your drinks: experiment and find out what works best for you.

Have an exit strategy

Before you go out, know how and when you're going to get home, whether it is by public transport, taxi or other means. Having your route home planned, ensures you don't have to rely on anyone else and takes the pressure off thinking you must stay all night. Pre-booked taxis are perfect for this as you can plan your exit time in advance and socialise on your own terms.

Remember: Once you realise that you can drink less alcohol and that you have got the willpower to do so, you will likely develop a new-found self-confidence. Being able to control the alcohol rather than the alcohol controlling you is a very powerful feeling. In a life with less alcohol, you feel a lot better; you wake up well rested, with no hangover and much more energy. You feel healthier physically and mentally. You will feel more confident and in control and ready to go to the next level.

25

FLEXIBILITY

Are your plans not working out? Learn to be flexible.

Our world is full of inflexible people who need to be in control. They take themselves too seriously and they take their plans too seriously. When we demonstrate a lack of flexibility, we create internal stress for ourselves, and to other people it comes across as annoying and selfish. There will always be times when our plans change due to unpredictable circumstances; things will get cancelled or someone will let us down or try to change everything. But is it worth getting upset over?

Insisting on getting what you want or adhering rigidly to your plans is often more stressful than going with the flow. Disruptions and variations to our plans will undoubtedly happen from time to time. When you learn to accept this fact and learn to go with the flow, you will become far more calm and relaxed. And those around you will feel more calm and relaxed too.

Here are some ways you can embrace flexibility in your life:

- Once you've made a decision or a plan, try to resist making detailed predictions in your mind as to how that decision or plan will pan out. You cannot predict the future so don't let your happiness depend on predicted outcomes.

- Be prepared for all eventualities.

- Always remember that you can modify a decision or plan at any time.

- Be willing to be wrong and be open to new ideas.

- Don't judge a situation too soon; instead, assess the situation thoroughly from all angles, analyse what you can retrieve or learn and then set new targets and make a new plan.

- Cultivate a positive expectancy of what will happen in the future no matter what problems arise. Every cloud!

Flexibility in the workplace creates a happier and more productive workforce, so organisations that let their employees shape their own jobs get more out of their staff. When staff are encouraged to fine-tune their role to fit their values, interests, strengths and skill set, they become much more motivated than if they had no choice in the matter.

Flexibility is also important when it comes to travelling. Travelling is a fantastic way to remove yourself from your daily routine and expose yourself to new experiences. When travelling, keep an open mind and don't plan for every single hour of your trip – leave plenty of time for random exploration of your surroundings and leave time to take advantage of new opportunities as they crop up.

Remember: Flexibility and patience in the pursuit of our goals will serve us well. In fact, we often learn the most from the biggest challenges we face. Planning is generally a good thing, but always be flexible if things don't go according to plan, and understand that unexpected twists and turns can actually deliver positive outcomes. For example, if you lose your job, you might choose a completely new career that ends up being much more fulfilling than your old one!

26

FAILURE

Are you making progress? Are you failing enough?!

Young children find it difficult to admit to their mistakes. They're programmed to deny any wrongdoing, even when the proof is undeniable. Unfortunately, as we mature into adults, we maintain this tendency and remain highly unwilling to acknowledge our mistakes or take criticism because it negatively affects our self-esteem. We therefore find it difficult to admit that we've made an error, especially when the error is a big one. We view failure as a personal shaming exercise. If left unchecked, this state of mind encourages us to play it safe, or in extreme cases it results in chronic risk aversion. We become too scared to try new things or take on new challenges, which hinders our ability to succeed.

Failure is often frustrating, but it's very important to realise that it's a crucial part of our development and growth. New and innovative ideas frequently occur when a certain failure or setback forces us to find a new approach. Failure is a vital part of our advancement, both personally and as a society.

Embrace failure

To realise your maximum potential, you must embrace failure. When low achievers fail, they often deny their mistakes by either blaming external circumstances or somehow concocting a way to recategorise a failure as a success. High achievers don't just recognise theoretically that failure is beneficial; they go one step further and form a very positive attitude toward it. When high achievers try something new and hit a few bumps in the road, they don't just give up. They learn how to avoid those road bumps next time round; they acknowledge their mistakes and look for different ways of doing it. Time after time they repeat this cycle.

People who can't cope with failure often choose to avoid it all costs, preferring to take an easier road over a bumpy one. In this way their fear of failure becomes a self-imposed obstacle to success – and is equivalent to failure in itself. For example, if you want to apply for a new job but your fear of failure prevents you from applying, then this is the same as failure. Or imagine you're in a social setting and want to chat to someone you like the look of, but your fear of rejection stops you. The outcome? Failure! And you didn't even give it your best shot. Another opportunity has passed you by.

The main advice here is simply to try. Get out of your comfort zone and give it a go. If things don't pan out, you'll gain useful feedback about what works and what doesn't and next time you can change your approach accordingly. Some things won't work out, but you'll miss out on some wonderful opportunities by not trying at all. People who see failure as a regular part of life are far less anxious about it because they've made a conscious decision to embrace it and use it as a stepping stone toward eventual success. This is an incredibly liberating insight.

Fail, fail and fail again

Take on new and exciting tasks each day and approach them with the mindset of an enthusiastic beginner. If you demonstrate a willingness to make mistakes, to improve and to acquire knowledge, you'll feel less pressure to perform. Oversights and errors will no longer be worrisome, but an expected, appreciated and useful part of the educational process. You can't avoid failure, so treat it as an essential aspect of your personal growth.

Many entrepreneurs are successful because of their resolute persistence after repeated failures. These people endure an average of 3.8 failed attempts before they hit upon a winning formula. They know that calculations, forecasts and predictions won't always prevent failure. When they encounter failure, they analyse the situation in detail and turn it into feedback which acts as a stimulant for new ideas. Many unexpected or unintended innovations and new ideas have materialised from problems and failures.

Try This: Look out for examples of failure that capture your imagination and motivate you. Find a suitable role model – a businessperson, sportsperson, entertainer or political figure – from which you can draw inspiration. Read up on their lives to find out about their failures as well as their successes.

People take various approaches to shield their self-image from failure, but the most common strategy is to simply sit on the fence and do nothing. These people say things like, 'I'm not failing because I'm incompetent; how can I be incompetent? I haven't even tried!' For these people failure negatively affects their self-esteem in a dramatic way and must be evaded, no matter what.

High achievers, on the other hand, spend much less time distressing about potential errors or problems; they just get on with the job. They put their best foot forward and do not overly concern themselves about the consequences if things go wrong. If they do fail, and many of them do at first, they will have a plan B and a plan C and so on. They do not give up at the first sign of failure.

Remember: Learn from your mistakes. Look at each decision as an exciting opportunity to approach life from a different angle. It's all a voyage of discovery, no matter which direction you choose to go. When you become confident that you can deal with a range of possible outcomes, both positive and negative, then you will be encouraged to try more things and take more risks. Mistakes will be made, that is for certain, but don't let this stop you from trying!

27

PERFECTION

Do you have a problem with perfectionism?

Are you a perfectionist? Do you think it's a positive quality to have?

Imagine you've completed 95 per cent of a new project at work or at home, yet you just can't finish it. Have you suddenly become lazy or incapable? Probably not – you might just be struggling with a dose of perfectionism. Some of us quote the following mantra to ourselves and others: 'If it's not perfect then it's not worth doing.' This is a very dangerous thought process because life is rarely perfect and if we restrict ourselves to perfect work, we may not complete anything.

Perfectionism sounds like a good thing, but it's likely to have a negative effect on your life. Perfectionism is different to simply trying your best and is very different to self-improvement. Perfectionists believe that if they appear perfect and behave perfectly, they'll avoid disapproval and humiliation. This mindset is unwholesome, however, because it means our happiness and self-respect depend on the opinion and endorsement of other people.

Some perfectionists believe that everything should be perfect, and they become frustrated when things aren't perfect. In chronic cases, perfectionism can lead to a form of inertia, whereby people avoid doing things or completing tasks due to fear of imperfection or fear of criticism. This outlook on life is also known as the 'not now' attitude: people are so afraid of failing due to the lack of a perfect strategy that when it's time to pull the trigger they keep saying, 'Not now'.

If we become too obsessed with having things done in a particular way, we're setting ourselves up for a life of disappointment. Perfectionists become fixated on what's wrong with things as opposed to what's good about them. Very few perfectionists have a relaxed and harmonious demeanour, because the very act of fixating on imperfection prevents them from appreciating and valuing the mostly imperfect world around them.

We live in a society where we vilify our heroes if they put a foot wrong. We scrutinise and dissect their every move, searching for imperfections and if we search hard enough, we're sure to find them. These people, many of which have done some great things, are not perfect because none of us are perfect!

Try This: If you're a perfectionist, try to adjust your outlook in the following ways:

- Be honest about your fear of criticism and shame.
- Don't let your imperfections define you.
- Instead of playing the 'not now' game, pull the trigger and see what happens without wasting time and energy worrying about imperfections.
- When you look in the mirror and all you see is imperfections, just go for a long walk in a crowded street and you'll see that you're surrounded by people who are just as imperfect. Maybe even more imperfect than you?
- Accept that life is often messy and then keep pushing on with your goals.
- Give yourself consent to be unexceptional or bad at some things – life is not a competition, so don't treat it as one. This attitude alone can be quite liberating.
- Stop wishing that everything should be better than it is, and gradually begin to accept that life is joyous and perfect the way it is. Without the opinion of a perfectionist, everything is usually fine.

Remember: Perfection rarely exists so don't let it get in the way of good or good enough. As you slowly release the necessity for perfection, you'll gradually see the joy of your imperfect life.

28

PERSPECTIVE

Are some things going wrong? Put everything into perspective!

Some people go through their lives experiencing enough hassle and frustration to fill 10 lifetimes. They get irritated and anxious about anything and everything: running late, other people running late, travel plans getting disrupted or someone saying or doing the wrong thing. In truth, we all do this from time to time – we lose perspective and create a major drama out of a minor problem. This type of overreaction is usually made worse if we've had a bad day or if we are in a foul mood.

Moods

Our good moods are associated with perspective and good judgement. During our good moods, life's tribulations are less intimidating, our interactions flow effortlessly, and we even take disapproval lightly. During our low moods, however, we change our perspective, and we start to believe that things are much worse than they actually are. We focus on everything that is wrong with ourselves and the world around us and we misunderstand people in negative ways. We take things personally and are easily offended.

The truth is, the world is the same and nothing has changed apart from our mood!

Be mindful that when you feel low, life is never as bad as it seems. The next time you find yourself in a bad mood, pay attention to your thought patterns. Don't forget that while your thoughts may be negative, your life probably hasn't changed that much, so challenge those thought patterns and try to think of a few positive things to focus on instead.

Everyone on this planet is less than perfect, so be more kind-hearted toward yourself and others and learn to accept the world as it is, including all those things that get on your nerves. Notice the pleasing and positive qualities of your surroundings, rather than fretting about the negative. The root of our bad moods is often a rigid refusal to allow things to be different to how we expected them to be, so managing your own expectations is crucial. How often do you hear the phrase 'it is what it is'? This saying is so common because it's simple and makes a lot of sense. The more we accept life's imperfections, without negative judgement, the more we'll feel relaxed and at peace with the world.

Expect less

Try This: Never assume that your taxi will arrive on time, or your urgent delivery will arrive when promised or that your builder will do a perfect job. Also, don't assume that the person at the other end of the phone when you complain will care that much either. They will have a different agenda and engaging sympathetically with your rage will not be part of it. Begin each day fully expecting that people or circumstances will occasionally let you down, especially those recognised trouble spots. You will then be mildly delighted when things go to plan, or you'll be less angry when they don't. Either way, you'll feel better.

Embrace life's problems

Try This: Try progressing through one week, fully expecting to encounter problems large and small. As difficulties arise, just calmly summarise and articulate each issue to yourself. Then consider the best way to approach it. If you regularly adopt this tactic, it will become a habit and you'll notice how relaxed and elegant each day can be. When we expect and embrace life's ups and downs rather than battling with them, we will enjoy life much more.

Reframe

Another powerful method which helps us break out of our established patterns of perception is reframing. There are numerous ways to look at life, and by reframing any given situation, you can view negative circumstances as positive.

For example, when you're annoyed that your tap is leaking, you might try thinking about how lucky you are to have clean running water delivered directly to your home. The same logic applies to your electricity supply and all the incredibly useful appliances that it powers. You're simply changing the frame of reference from negative to positive.

As another example, you could reframe 'nervousness' as 'excitement'. When you next feel anxious about something, such as an important meeting or speaking in front of a large group, don't worry too much about calming down – use your anxiety to your advantage instead. Being nervous puts you in a state of physical and mental alertness and anticipation, so instead of being scared, tell yourself that you're excited and ready. This positive substitute for fear will help you appear calm and in control, and once you get started everything will fall into place.

Compare your reaction to that of others

No two people will react to adversity in the same way. When you get yourself worked up by an unfortunate situation in your life, it might be worth performing a simple reality check. For example, if your home is subject to water damage due to a burst pipe, and this is making you incredibly angry and sad, try comparing your reaction to that of some other people you know. How would a particular friend or sibling react, or what about the kind lady across the road? I cannot guarantee that their reactions would be less extreme than yours, but I can guarantee that they will be different. This thought experiment won't solve your problem, but it will add a little perspective to your reaction to it.

Remember: As Mark Twain once said, 'Life is just one damn thing after another', and if we fight against this natural law, we're setting ourselves up for misery. If, on the other hand, you can come to terms with this, you'll feel fine every time the pendulum swings from good times to bad. And remember, not getting what you want is sometimes a wonderful stroke of luck because your biggest challenges are often your greatest opportunities.

29

ENJOYMENT

Don't forget to have some fun!

Many of us plan our lives far too vigorously, which often leaves us feeling bad about not having time for a little bit of fun and enjoyment. The way we live our lives is defined by the way we live each day. And each day is just a compilation of little moments, one after another. Only you can select how you approach each of these moments: with a negative disposition or with a positive, cheerful demeanour. Instead of approaching seemingly mundane activities with the same old negative attitude, try to introduce a little fun into the process.

Goals you'll enjoy

When you think of your goals (see Chapter 7), do you associate them with fun and enjoyment, or do you associate them with discipline, discomfort, austerity and drudgery? I ask this question because researchers have discovered that the two decisive factors in reaching a goal are how satisfying you find doing the necessary tasks and what you achieve at each stage of the process. As you might expect, when you enjoy your goal *and* the tasks it requires, you have the best formula for success.

When setting your goals, it's important, therefore, to ask yourself not only what you truly want but exactly *why* you want it. Keep asking yourself this 'Why?' question until you're fully satisfied that your goals are chosen for the right reasons.

Next, you need to make the journey to those goals as much fun as possible. This is easy if your goal is to visit the theatre more often, but not so easy when it comes to things like running every day to improve your physical fitness. In this example, you might find your initial training runs hard work and boring, and not exactly fun! You might need to be more creative in order to build in as much fun as possible. For example, rather than simply running to keep fit, why not play a sport like tennis, badminton, squash, volleyball, netball or football, or try swimming, martial arts or cycling?

Rewards

Sometimes, essential tasks are hard work or boring no matter how you tweak them. In these cases, you could introduce an element of fun by giving yourself some rewards along the way. Let's say your goal is to lose weight. This type of goal can either be driven by fear of failure or by rewards, and the latter is a lot more fun! So try to incorporate small but meaningful and fun rewards when you reach short-term goals. This could be a visit to your favourite restaurant or going to see the latest movie release. To get the most happiness from your rewards, anticipate them before they unfold, and recall them often.

Deadlines

Some people dislike deadlines, but they can be a source of enjoyment because you get an exhilarating feeling when you meet them. Therefore, instead of setting a single monthly deadline, try setting small deadlines every day to get a regular 'deadline rush' that keeps you motivated.

Do what you love

What precisely do you enjoy doing? One way to help you identify what you enjoy the most is to make a list of all your activities and then rate them all by level of enjoyment. Based on these results, try to avoid activities near the bottom and do more of the activities near the top. Be sure to try new things too because novelty itself is a major source of fun and joy.

Work life balance

Setting aside time for the activities we enjoy is often difficult to prioritise because we tend to attach self-esteem to sheer productivity. We think of work and play as being mutually exclusive, so we forgo relaxation, recreation and sometimes our health if they interfere with our work. But leisure time encourages people to experience freedom, which often leads to feelings of control, competence, and improved self-esteem, and to deprive ourselves of these can lead to negative consequences such as stress and burnout. Paradoxically, if you increase the amount of leisure and relaxation you give yourself, you can become more industrious. Regular time off will bring a sense of enthusiasm and freshness back to your work while also nurturing compassion and originality.

Laugh a little more

In the early days of human history, laughter developed as a linguistic device to relieve stress and let people know that everything was okay. In modern times we laugh to let other people know how we're feeling, usually as a result of positive emotional states such as joy, happiness or relief. Laughter can also make upsetting situations easier to cope with because it suppresses tension and worry. Communicating our problems to other people through jokes and humour allows us to recognise our fears and connect with other humans without getting morose.

Laughter also has beneficial effects on our health. It has been shown to lead to reductions in stress hormones such as cortisol and epinephrine and to boost the immune system. Laughter and cheerfulness are social emotions associated with bonding, agreement, affection and of course, humour. Laughter makes life fun and can diminish feelings of anxiety, pain, irritation, sadness, shame and failure. Being cheerful means you're choosing to live a joyful life, while spreading a feeling of happiness to everyone around you.

Remember: Try to make joy, happiness, fun and laughter priorities. Expect to feel good and pay more attention to the best that can happen, not the worst that can happen. Remain on the lookout for things that make you laugh or try to be funny yourself. Laugh and smile as often as possible. Laugh at yourself – your friends will love you for it. Have fun!

30

PUBLIC SPEAKING

How do you handle giving a speech or presentation?

Public speaking is one of the most dreaded forms of communication I can think of, but when you do it and you do it well, it can be immensely rewarding. Aside from the feel-good factor and pure relief that it's all over, public speaking allows us to form connections, influence decisions and motivate change. Many of us lack the confidence to speak in front of a large group of people and we spend our lives avoiding it all costs. However, I can highly recommend having a try at some point, so in this chapter I've compiled a few handy tips to guide you through the process.

What is the point of your speech?

The first question you need to ask yourself is why your target audience should listen to you? In truth, there are probably many reasons why people should listen to you but be mindful of this question throughout the planning process.

If your speech is of an informal or entertaining nature, such as a wedding speech or a few words at a special occasion, then be sure to prepare more than you think you need to prepare. Very few of us can successfully pull off this kind of speech 'off the cuff', so do a few trial runs before the event. Your speech will be specific and personal to you, your audience and your style, but this type of speech is usually a mix of sincerity and humour. Do your homework: there are many books and web sources that are dedicated to helping people write wedding speeches, for example, so I recommend researching before you start writing.

The rest of this chapter is devoted to the process of delivering more formal speeches or presentations as part of your work or studies.

Start strong

Start by telling your audience who you are and why you're speaking to them. To get their attention quickly, introduce your key message straight away. If this key message is attention grabbing and serves to build anticipation, you're off to a great start. Here are a few ways to get your audience's attention:

- **State that there's something important they need to hear about.** This will generate intrigue and heightened attentiveness as they eagerly await the new information.
- **Illustrate your key message with an inspiring and motivating story.** For example, you could tell your team

about another company or organisation that used to be in your current situation and went on to do great things.

- **Share an interesting fact or a surprising statistic.**
- **Inject some humour.**

Keep it short and focused

Be careful not to bore your audience with too much background information, and don't overwhelm them with too many new ideas. Try to limit your speech to around 15 minutes; keep it simple and relevant, and finish with an unforgettable one-liner that is closely linked to the key message you gave at the beginning.

Use visuals

Studies have shown that 65 per cent of us prefer to learn visually. The statistics show that we recall:

- 80 per cent of what we see
- 30 per cent of what we read
- 10 percent of what we hear

For this reason, be sure to use attention grabbing visual aids to emphasise your ideas. Graphics, film clips, diagrams and pictures can get your message across much more effectively than just words. Keep these simple, however, because too much information crammed onto one infographic will confuse your audience or send them to sleep. Also, try to incorporate unusual and innovative content that surprises your audience and stimulates their curiosity. Engaging audio or video recordings, humorous images and quirky props are all good examples.

Language and rhythm

Think about the rhythm of your speech. Switch between short, bold sentences and longer, more detailed sentences. A strategically placed pause can be very effective to emphasise an important point. This adds weight to what you've just said and adds an extra few seconds to let it sink in. (That said, you don't want any long silences after you've invited the audience to ask questions, so have your own questions ready just in case nobody asks one!)

Tune in to the melodic qualities of some of your words. Rhyming words, alliteration and repetition are your friends, and they'll make your speech more entertaining and more memorable.

Edit your final draft until it sounds like everyday language and allow plenty of rehearsal time. Given adequate practice, you'll only need to look at your notes every now and again. Being well prepared and well-rehearsed will help you iron out any mistakes, find a good rhythm and calm any nerves.

Stir emotions

The best speeches create an emotional response in the audience which gets them primed for a compelling call to action at the end. When language stirs our emotions, it carries more weight and lives longer in the memory. There are many ways of achieving this, but the most common way is to use metaphors and stories:

- **Metaphors** are potent because they capture our attention while simplifying complex ideas. A simple metaphor, such as 'Time is money', can create a vivid and memorable connection in the brain. An expanded metaphor can initiate a stream of memorable pictures in your listeners' heads: 'If we sow these seeds now, the roots will soon take hold, and this time next year our garden will be blooming!'

- A carefully thought-out **story** makes it easier to organise our thoughts and make sense of complicated issues. Stories have a subtle, yet big impact because they captivate and motivate your audience, while entertaining them at the same time.

Another technique for stirring emotions and maintaining attention levels is to ask your audience a question every now and again. Asking a question that invites an immediate answer helps your audience to establish their own narrative, and they'll be far more convinced by this narrative than if you'd stated it for them.

Passion and positivity

According to Chris Anderson, curator of the TED conference, the most successful TED talks are delivered by speakers who have a passion for their idea and consequently deliver their talks with emotion and imagination.

If passionate speaking doesn't come naturally to you, you can learn this skill through observation and practice. Observe passionate speakers and mimic their various techniques until you find what works for you. Use your body, hands and facial expressions, adding colour and emotion to draw your audience in to your story.

Smile as much as you can; it's the easiest way to appear relaxed and self-assured, and to convey friendliness. Make eye contact whenever possible too, as it makes you come across as considerate, honest and genial.

Remember: Whether you're speaking in front of a small team at work or a much larger audience, it can go well or go badly. Your performance has a major impact on how you're judged as an individual, which is why it can cause excessive worry and nervousness. With thorough preparation and rehearsal, however, you will overcome your nerves and stand the best chance of success.

31

INSPIRATION

Need some inspiration? Go and seek it out!

Are you bored or stuck in a rut? Or short on ideas? Then you might need some inspiration. Inspiration can convert apathy into curiosity and redirect you toward new possibilities. Inspiration allows us to surpass our day-to-day experiences and limitations. It gives us both the enthusiasm and resources to break down barriers, be creative and grow closer to our goals. It encourages us to learn from and collaborate with others.

But what if there is no inspiration? Then you must go and actively search for it. Inspiration is usually the result of a new idea or concept, but when it comes to having good ideas, there's no precise recipe – the secret is to actively and deliberately generate them – lots of them! For most of us, good ideas don't always appear that easily; they need to be actively sought after, worked on, nurtured and given time to develop into the finished article.

Put your ideas down on paper

If you already have some promising ideas and plans jumbled up in your head, get those ideas written down so you can articulate and evaluate them more precisely. When you first have an idea, it begins life as an assortment of imprecise thoughts and possible outcomes. Writing the idea down helps you define it in more detail and helps you identify any flawed assumptions or missing information.

Try Brainstorming

You can brainstorm in a group or on your own, and the only rule that applies is that there are no strict rules. In a brainstorming session, the basic process is to fire out as many ideas as possible without judging those ideas. Everything should be written down without editing. This isn't the time to judge or reject ideas. They all have equal weight and quantity trumps quality at this stage. Brainstorming is a popular creative practice because it helps to generate new ideas while suppressing internal and external criticism. Brainstorming encourages the creative and inventive part of the mind to consider new ideas that we might usually reject.

In 1968, George Land conducted a research study to test the creativity of 1,600 children aged between three and five years old.

He retested the same children at 10 years of age and again at 15. The results were amazing:

- Creativity amongst 5-year-olds: 98%
- Creativity amongst 10-year-olds: 30%
- Creativity amongst 15-year-olds: 12%
- Creativity amongst adults: 2%

Our education system was designed during the industrial revolution two to three hundred years ago to try to make us into good workers who follow instructions. For most of us our creativity has been buried under a plethora of rules, memorised information and procedures. We therefore need to encourage our inner child to influence our thinking during the brainstorming process.

Why not make a wish? Children say things like 'I wish I could float in the air' or 'I wish I could drive an F1 car'. From the hot-air balloon to video games to F1 simulators, many youthful fantasies have been transposed into exciting creations.

When brainstorming, the more ideas you produce, the better. By creating a large quantity of ideas, you'll have a higher probability of developing a few great ideas. Even if your ideas seem ridiculous, keep playing with them and tweaking them – without realising it, you might be close to that 'eureka' moment.

Creativity is more about breaking rules than following them. Think about some of the most successful people in the world. Are they careful and diligent rule-followers? Certainly not; they're motivated by new ideas rather than outdated rules because they know that too many rules stifle possibility. If everyone followed the rules all the time, invention and advancement would be at an end.

Expand on an idea

Another good way to stimulate your idea factory is to take something that's been done and either expand on it or take it in a different direction. For instance, there are many scientific papers and specialist magazines containing fascinating ideas that have been overlooked. The internet is also a mine of information if you look in the right places. What other information sources, contacts or old ideas have you left unexploited? By adapting current ideas and other stimuli that are thought-provoking and relevant, you might unearth all kinds of possibilities.

Look to solve a problem

Everyday frustrations can act as stepping stones to products that solve common problems. Pay close attention to things that aren't quite right and begin formulating solutions. How can existing technology be slightly modified to find game-changing ideas? Can you borrow bits and pieces of other people's ideas?

Use your subconscious

Your subconscious mind is very much an unknown quantity, but it is a powerful tool. Scientists still don't fully know exactly how our brain works but your subconscious and intuitive mind can be used to help disentangle and solve daily problems. First you must spend a little 'conscious' time analysing the problem, talking to others and making a list of possible solutions with associated pros and cons. Then take your mind off the problem completely and let your brain go to work in the background. The answer might take some time, but it will come eventually.

Collaborate

If all the above advice sounds a little daunting, or if you are struggling to make any progress, try drafting in a little help from other people. Find people who know how to think out of the box. Be open to their suggestions and throw a few ideas around without imposing too many boundaries. They might help you discover a new angle that stimulates some great ideas!

Remember: Successful individuals don't necessarily come up with their ideas straight away; more often than not they develop by accumulating many small insights over time. And the more you search for inspiration, the more chance you have of finding it.

32

KNOWLEDGE

You can't evolve in a vacuum. Expand your field of knowledge.

If you didn't learn any new information or acquire any new skills in the next decade, how relevant and useful would your current skill set be in 10 years' time? Not very! We need to keep learning and progressing, continually acquiring new knowledge and expertise; otherwise our competence and resulting confidence levels will plummet.

Learning isn't just about maintaining competence – acquiring new knowledge also helps us make the innovative connections needed for inspiration (see Chapter 31). Learning earns us the respect of others and helps us to collaborate with them. And it can make us feel good about ourselves!

Be a willing learner

Ultimately, an enthusiasm to learn is the pathway to achievement. High achievers are continually acquiring more skills and new information. They read about people they look up to and submerge themselves in numerous realms of knowledge. People with higher levels of curiosity are generally more successful, simply because they're prepared to learn more than everyone else.

Cast your net wide

Your career might make it necessary to keep abreast of the latest advances being made in your field of business, but that doesn't mean you should concentrate your learning on a narrow bracket of highly specialised information. The multifaceted fields of history, technology, art and science, for example, can be studied and valued by any of us.

Plan your learning

Try This: To formalise the learning process, you can make a yearly learning schedule. I suggest the following allocation of time:

- 30 per cent for new knowledge relevant to your specific business field

- 30 per cent for non-essential things that will help you in a broader sense, such as learning new languages or career skills not specific to your area of expertise such as accountancy or marketing

- 40 per cent for things you're fascinated by, such as travel, cooking, wildlife or sport.

Every now and again, try to branch out and read something completely different – a little poetry with a glass of wine might be fun! Review your plan regularly and tweak the percentages according to your current needs and preferences. Use the internet – there's masses of free stuff out there – and listen to some educational podcasts.

Tread carefully online

The internet is obviously a great source of information – but beware! Because it's open and unregulated, ensuring the accuracy of information might be a problem. Anyone can post anything on the internet, so there'll always be a small percentage of biased, inaccurate and false information. Many websites encourage everyone to share their thoughts, which enables thousands of overconfident individuals to analyse and comment on complex issues without having any relevant knowledge.

Ask an expert

You can learn many things on your own, but be careful if you need specialised information, or accountancy, legal or medical advice.

In these instances, be sure to ask a professional who's qualified to help you. Many of us try to teach ourselves, or we ask a friend who's simply not experienced enough to advise us.

Remember: The power of education and knowledge will positively impact your growth and development. It will influence everything in your life including relationships, hobbies and your career. It will make you wise enough to make many more decisions independently; decisions that will help you progress and achieve your goals.

33

BIASES

Question what you know and identify what you don't know.

Our brains are capable of some highly sophisticated thinking, but they're also capable of taking some highly unsophisticated shortcuts. Some of these shortcuts, evolved by early humans, helped us make urgent, quick decisions, such as what to do when we experience danger. In modern times, however, most of these shortcuts are caused by our lazy brains searching for as much simplicity as possible. In these situations, our thinking becomes illogical and flawed by what social scientists call biases. Some of the most common biases are outlined in the paragraphs below.

Attribution bias

Most people have a tendency to attribute their achievements to their own talent, but attribute their flops to outside forces. This attribution bias is typical of a general overconfidence bias, whereby we generally overrate our own ability. How many people would state that they were a below-average driver or state that they were an above-average driver? Most people would rate themselves as above average, but the truth is that 50 per cent are above average and 50 per cent are below average. Most people think they're more exceptional than they actually are, and they see their day-to-day activities as more important than those that happen to other people.

Direction dependency bias

The direction from which we arrive at a given outcome influences how good we feel about it. For example, if I won £600 today and lost £500 tomorrow, I would be less happy than if I had simply won £100 tomorrow, even though the final outcome is the same.

The direction dependency bias is the reason why we adhere to existing opinions even when new and compelling information comes to light. It also lies behind the *halo effect*, which is the tendency to like (or dislike) a person, organisation or situation, no matter what. Once we like a person, for example, we tend to cling on to that opinion because the halo effect disproportionately prioritises the importance of first impressions.

Framing bias

We easily succumb to the framing bias because alternative ways of presenting the same facts arouse different emotions: '90 per cent sugar free' sounds better than '10 per cent sugar'.

Hindsight bias

Hindsight bias, also known as the 'knew-it-all-along' bias, is the propensity we have when we perceive past events as having been more foreseeable than they actually were. Almost all outcomes are predictable with the benefit of hindsight, and unfortunately this encourages over-optimism in our capacity to foresee how events will pan out in the future. Hindsight bias may also cause distortions of memories of what was known or believed before an event occurred.

With hindsight, we also confuse the quality of our decisions with the quality of their consequences. Some of our bad decisions can actually lead to good things and some of our good decisions can lead to bad things. The truth is, our decisions are rarely totally right or totally wrong, but somewhere in between. Decisions are usually made with incomplete information, including some known unknowns and a number of unknown unknowns.

The Planning Fallacy

The planning fallacy is a phenomenon in which predictions about how much time will be needed to complete a future project are underestimated. Business plans, for example, are often based on wishful thinking rather than a credible assessment of likelihoods. They overrate progress and profits and underrate problems and losses. Overconfident planners will emphasise scenarios of success, while downplaying the possibility of failure.

Availability bias

With this bias, we attach disproportionate weight to recent information, especially if it's quite dramatic. For example, a recent plane disaster will alter our thoughts about the safety of flying for a few days or weeks – a view often intensified by massive news coverage. The truth is that fatalities from illness are 20 times more likely than fatalities from accidents, but accidents are more newsworthy so our fear of them is disproportionally high.

Loss aversion bias

Loss aversion is a term used to describe a person's inclination to prefer avoiding losses to receiving equivalent gains – for most of us it's better to not lose £50 than to gain £50. When it comes to personal finances, loss aversion bias prevents investors from making reasonable investments. Loss aversion also explains why we don't take that new job or start that new business venture, instead preferring to continue with our current situation.

Confirmation bias

Confirmation bias, coined by English psychologist Peter Wason, is the tendency of people to favour information that confirms and strengthens their established beliefs, while ignoring or rejecting evidence that supports a different viewpoint. While we can't avoid confirmation bias entirely, we can minimise it by expanding our knowledge base and making a conscious effort to see every issue from multiple viewpoints. This is the essence of critical thinking.

We don't know how much we don't know

Knowing a few facts about a particular subject often doesn't reduce our conviction that we fully understand that subject. This is called The Dunning–Kruger effect. The less knowledge we have makes it easier to apply that knowledge into a coherent narrative even though it can be wildly inaccurate.

We have instinctive thoughts and attitudes about many things. We take a liking or disliking to certain individuals when we know little about them. We put the world to rights, drawing opinions based on flimsy evidence that we don't fully comprehend. We rely on and overrate our common sense. Common sense is something we trust for many daily decisions, but all too often, it's woefully insufficient as it fails to tackle more complicated issues with many interconnected variables.

When we understand the weaknesses of common sense and the other biases mentioned in this chapter, we can make more considered decisions and more robust plans for future events and projects. All of our life events and acquired knowledge are stored away in our brains for future use, but over time, they get altered, oversimplified or simply forgotten. We might think we have enough knowledge or experience to execute any given plan, but we must always develop and refine that knowledge by consulting experts, questioning our biases and pursuing information that will further boost our understanding and capabilities.

Remember: The world in your mind isn't an exact version of the real world. Much of our thinking consists of wild generalisations and assumptions. We often feel we can override realistic probabilities because we have superior intelligence or 'intuition'. Beware of this fallacy because that's how mistakes are made. Replace anecdotal or biased thinking with critical and statistical reasoning based on well-researched facts and figures. Make statistics your friend. Question what you know, be aware of what you don't know and get informed!

34

THOUGHTS AND EMOTIONS

What are you thinking and feeling? Observe your thoughts.

Our thoughts and emotions can be both a strength and a weakness. Our mind can spawn great initiatives, but it can also get in the way and block our progress. Our brain is fallible in many ways, so let's begin by looking at three common unhelpful thought patterns that we all experience.

Thought attacks

Have you ever observed how anxious you feel when you get fixated on a negative train of thought? You start speculating about imaginary scenarios and one negative thought feeds into another and another and so on, until you're tense and troubled. When this type of 'thought attack' takes hold, it's difficult to feel calm, let alone resourceful.

Ruminating about social affairs

We often find ourselves absent-mindedly daydreaming about our interactions with various people in our lives. Unfortunately, we tend to spend more time preoccupied with the downside of many of our personal relationships than with the upside. We negatively speculate about a message unanswered, a call not returned or a conversation that didn't go well. Our imagination blows things out of proportion by creating a number of mental scenarios that cause nothing but worry and anxiety. Social interaction is essential for most of us, so it's no surprise that we feel upset when things go wrong or if we are worried that something might go wrong in our social lives.

Negative thinking

What you feel inside – contentment, discontentment, joy, sadness, elation, misery, love or hatred – is the direct consequence of how you communicate with yourself. Your state of mind isn't the result of what's happening in your life but your interpretation of what's happening. The stories the mind manufactures are rarely accurate, and when it distorts reality in a negative way, it produces negative emotions. This is the essence of negative thinking.

Research shows that our brains have evolved to respond a lot more intensely to negative experiences and interactions than positive ones. We tend to focus on the negative even when those negative consequences are trivial. This tendency varies from person to person and is highly dependent on a part of the brain called the amygdala, which takes care of our emotional responses.

Neuroplasticity

The ability of neural networks in the brain to change through growth and reorganisation is called neuroplasticity, and fortunately the amygdala can learn to be happier with a little training. Psychologists spend many hours walking their patients through psychological exercises, which with repetition can slowly alter the brain's biochemistry and configuration. By positively focusing their attention, they're able to expose deceptive messages and improve their brain's ability to feel contentment.

Three steps to improve your thinking

Step 1: Observe

Simply trying to suppress negative emotions doesn't work – the emotions always reappear, often with higher intensity. We therefore need to firstly acknowledge and accept their existence, and then try to identify their root cause, which means trying to observe and understand what the mind is doing as it's doing it.

Try This: The process of observing your own mind is sometimes referred to as mindfulness, and it requires some effort and practice. Here's an exercise for initiating mindfulness: Find a quiet place with a comfortable seat, close your eyes and focus all your concentration on your breathing. Observe your thoughts and emotions as they enter and leave your consciousness. Notice them, but don't analyse or judge them. If you catch yourself thinking too much, refocus your concentration back to your breathing. The goal at this stage is to gain an awareness of your thought processes without assigning opinions or making any decisions. Try to do this a few times a day for several days.

Once you get comfortable with the mindfulness exercise, you'll naturally be curious about what messages these thoughts or emotions are offering you. Ask yourself:

- Am I thinking about unpleasant events from the past?
- Am I worried about what might happen in the future?
- How do my thoughts make me feel?
- How would I like to feel?
- What can I learn from these thoughts?

Step 2: Analyse

Identify exactly what you're thinking or feeling. For example, make sure you haven't confused a feeling of anger with a feeling of disappointment or pain. Listen to what your thoughts and emotions are trying to tell you. Pay attention to them in the same way that you would pay attention to a friend confiding in you. When you've listened to them and acknowledged them, you'll find your thoughts and feelings will lower their intensity and you'll be able to move forward with more clarity and calmness.

Try to identify repeated thought patterns and then label them. For example, is your mind spinning, ruminating, worrying or wandering? This will help you understand how your brain is currently working. When you can identify and label your thoughts, you're more able to change your relationship with them in a constructive way.

One common thinking error is binary thinking, which involves labelling situations at the extremes, such as 'perfect' or 'awful'. Another error is catastrophising, which entails blowing your current situation out of proportion or foreseeing that something awful is about to happen. If you overanalyse things, or engage in excessive 'what if' thinking, this will often lead you down the road to catastrophising.

Try This: At this stage it's useful to write down all the key thoughts, feelings and emotions that you experience each day. Also write down the events or circumstances that cause these thoughts and emotions. Are there any repetitive themes that jump out at you? The simple process of writing down exactly what is happening inside your mind is incredibly liberating in its own right. Give it a try.

Step 3: Change your mind

Once you've observed and analysed your thought patterns, devote some time to actively changing them and rewiring your brain for more positive thinking. This means evaluating situations from a much broader and more optimistic perspective, rather than from a narrow and negative perspective. Begin to care for yourself and others. Make choices with a calm, compassionate and loving frame of mind, rather than one of anxiety, jealousy, hatred or rage.

Try This: Cultivate a pre-emptive strategy to deal with repetitive negative thought patterns that need to be challenged. Can you re-evaluate these thoughts by looking at them from different perspectives? How would someone else evaluate your thoughts? Do you need to tweak the vocabulary you use to explain these thoughts? What other thoughts could you have instead?

As you work on changing your mind, try to do the following:

- **Don't daydream about your problems – look for solutions instead.** Think back to when you successfully dealt with a similar problem before. Recollect how you were effective in the past and how that might help you handle the current problem. Write down a few possible solutions and work out the best course of action. When things work out well don't forget to give yourself a pat on the back – success breeds confidence so acknowledge it when it happens.

- **Avoid blame.** Don't always blame external forces for your negative thoughts and feelings. That said, there are always occasions when someone oversteps the mark, and you have a genuine grievance. But don't forget that only you can control your thinking or your mood, so always try to stay calm and write down a few possible courses of action. And if this doesn't work, don't blame yourself for not being in control – you're doing the best you can with what you have.

- **Take responsibility.** Are you playing the victim role? Are you taking responsibility for your thoughts and feelings? If things are spiralling out of control, step back and return to 'Step 1' above.

- **Be your own best friend.** After you've been through the exercises above a few times, you'll recognise that the biggest problem of all is your negative internal chatterbox! Try everything you can to swap this pessimist for a caring and more upbeat internal companion.

- **Talk to yourself.** Speaking your thoughts out loud can help you clarify your thought processes more effectively than just thinking about your thoughts. Self-talk can help you think more clearly, evaluate situations with more certainty and therefore make decisions more easily. Giving yourself an occasional motivational pep talk can also break down a few mental barriers and help you move forward. Speaking to yourself sympathetically will also have a positive influence on your overall mental well-being.

Once you get more experience of going through this process, you'll begin to observe your negative thinking before it has a chance to grow in intensity. The earlier you catch yourself, the simpler it will be to consciously take your thoughts in a more constructive direction. In time your mini successes will build on themselves. You'll observe your negative thoughts more often and be wise enough to recognise that it's only your thinking that's distressing you, not the real world!

Divert your attention

If you get stuck in a rut and the steps in the previous section aren't working, take a break and divert your attention toward a fun or constructive activity for a while. You could go for a mindful walk, concentrating only on your body movement, your breathing and the sights and sounds around you. You could exercise, spend time on a hobby, talk to a friend or just put your feet up and watch a little TV. Don't try to actively eradicate your upsetting thoughts; this exercise is about allowing them to be present but reducing their intensity for a while with a few pleasant distractions.

Put on a pair of rose-tinted glasses

Our memories of past events distort and fragment as time passes by, and we later reassemble them inaccurately, viewing them through the lens of our current values and philosophies. Those of us who have positive recollections of past events are prone to be more content, healthful and successful than people with negative recollections of the past. Amazingly, this still holds true when those memories are flimsy or wildly wrong.

Try This: We can simulate this attitude by making a regular habit of writing down a few things from the past that have made us happy. If you look upon these events with gratitude, you'll give an extra boost to the positive feelings they create inside. It's impossible to alter the past, but it is possible to improve our relationship with it.

Reasons to be cheerful

Train your brain to deliberately notice the positive facets of life. Notice the beautiful sky, the beauty of nature and notice the positive aspects of the people around you. When you've finished one of your daily tasks, however large or small, always stop and give yourself a virtual pat on the back. Always be on the lookout for these positive moments – they won't change the world, but they will change how you look at it.

Try This: Make time to write down a few pleasant things that you notice each day. Be on the lookout for reasons to be happy, not reasons to be unhappy. Are in good health? Do you have a roof over your head? Do you have some nice food in the house? Do you have some nice clothes? These are basic requirements but not everyone can answer yes to all these questions – think of those people who are much worse off than you. This will help you take the edge off any negativity by redirecting your mind toward basic comforts and maybe even small luxuries that you can be thankful for.

Look for positive experiences

Since the conscious brain has a negative bias, we must continually work at remaining upbeat and allowing time for positive interactions. Try to think of new positive experiences to engage with. Share your positive experiences with those around you and be genuinely happy for them when they share their positive experiences with you. Our thoughts and feelings are derived from our life experiences, so by seeking nurturing and positive experiences, we are laying the emotional foundations for a happier future.

Are you depressed?

Those suffering from depression often get caught in a repetitive cycle of ruminating about things that make them more depressed. They incessantly fixate on past negative experiences, ensuring a constant stream of negative thinking that makes them miserable and depressed. If you're having serious problems with negative thinking and painful emotions, seek the advice of a medical professional or counsellor. Don't try to get through it on your own. Qualified mental health practitioners with years of study, training and experience, are ready and able to help you.

Remember: Becoming happier isn't a matter of ridding yourself of negative thoughts – you're bound to have them from time to time. What matters is how we handle our thoughts.

According to an article published by the National Science Foundation of the USA, the average person has around 12,000 to 60,000 thoughts per day. 80 per cent of those thoughts are negative and 95 per cent are the same thoughts as the day before. What an incredible waste of mental energy!

Rather than getting caught in this overthinking and overanalysing mental merry-go-round, try to consciously control and direct your thinking in more constructive ways and become the master of your mind. A thought is only a thought; a chemical reaction in our brain, and it's unable to harm us without our permission.

35

FEEDBACK AND CRITICISM

We all love compliments. But how do you react to negative feedback?

Most people only receive formal feedback in their work environment, which is generally considered to be a beneficial process both for the employee and the business. In fact, one of the best tools to improve any business is a robust performance appraisal structure, whereby managerial staff are encouraged to give detailed feedback to employees. In addition, studies have shown that offering regular and considered feedback is highly connected to employee enthusiasm as it helps them learn, improve and flourish.

Most businesses also actively seek feedback from their customers and other stakeholders. They're particularly interested in complaints and negative feedback, which give them a better understanding of their performance and how they can improve.

Clearly, businesses value feedback, but what about individuals? Positive feedback is usually no problem, but when it comes to negative feedback, we're often less open because we don't like to disclose our flaws or limitations – it's not a conversation we enjoy. This attitude is unlikely to help us grow and achieve our goals; we will benefit much more by assessing all aspects of ourselves, especially those flaws and limitations.

It's useful, therefore, to consider some coping mechanisms for when criticism is aimed in your direction, and it's even more useful to develop a mindset that proactively seeks feedback, both positive and negative.

Expect your share of criticism

If you place a high value on admiration, you equate your self-worth directly to the amount of approval or disapproval you receive from other people. This craving for approval, however, will sometimes make you unhappy because your sense of well-being will depend entirely on how people respond to you. A disrespectful comment, for example, can either result in unwarranted self-doubt or provoke unpleasant feelings of annoyance or hurt.

We all have personal standards by which we appraise our lives and the lives of others, and our standards won't always correlate with everyone else's. Many of us are easily offended by the smallest

214

criticism or disapproval. We feel as if our whole being is under attack, so we get defensive or counter-attack, or both. Responding in this way, however, takes a huge toll on our emotional energy and stress levels, so we need another strategy.

We need to learn to take all forms of disapproval with a pinch of salt. It really doesn't matter that much if you don't impress every single person you encounter. In fact, if you expect and anticipate the occasional disapproving comments, you'll negotiate life much more smoothly. The key takeaway here is that you can't please all of the people all of the time – so don't even bother trying.

Listen rather than argue

Criticism can be very emotive, so when you encounter it try to reign in your defensive reflexes. If you get angry and go on the offensive, the other person will be annoyed that you're contradicting them and they're likely to hold onto their position with even more hostility. To break this cycle:

- Notice and acknowledge your anger but set it aside for a minute. Stay calm and try not to say too much.
- The other person might be angry themselves, so focus on the words being spoken, not the way they're communicated.
- Listen carefully, ask questions and try to understand the criticism being offered. This will take the heat out of the situation.

- After careful consideration, make your response in a calm tone of voice.

A morsel of truth

We've all been guilty of thinking we're right when we're wrong, but how we approach circumstances in which we realise we're wrong speaks volumes about our trustworthiness, honesty and readiness to learn from our mistakes. Not everyone finds that this comes naturally, usually because their ego gets in the way. If this describes you, I strongly recommend that you turn over a new leaf and become totally honest with yourself and the world.

A good starting point is to proactively accept and agree with some of the disapproval that comes your way. You won't feel like doing this every time and you don't have to agree with everything, but at least consider it as an option. The benefits of this strategy are:

- It will cool things down a little.
- It will satisfy the others person's desire to articulate their opinions.
- It will demonstrate that you've taken on board what the other person has had to say.
- It gives you the chance to understand your weaknesses a little better.

Seek honest feedback

Once you're comfortable with receiving negative feedback, go out into the world and actively seek more of it. While we all enjoy positive feedback, an overabundance of praise can result in you no longer being motivated to improve, so approach people you trust and ask them specifically for some negative feedback. Ask questions that push the responses toward your weaknesses, such as, 'Where is my biggest blind spot?' and 'How can I improve XYZ?' The more accurate the answers, the better, so make it okay for them to give you some constructive criticism. The more feedback you can get, the better, so seek it out from many diverse sources.

Give yourself feedback

Try This: Why not write down your strengths and weaknesses as you see them? What do you think you need to do differently? Have a good think about your life in general. Make a list of the things you like and don't like about it. Then, where feasible, prioritise changing the things you dislike while trying to do more of the things you like. Make this a continuous process. For example, each evening check in with yourself. How did you act and how did you feel during the day? What went well? What didn't go so well and how can you change your approach next time?

Try not to criticise others

Are you always on the lookout for the imperfections in people and the mistakes they make? This habit might make you feel superior, but when you pick fault in anyone and everyone around you, it says more about you than it does about them. Giving carefully thought-out constructive criticism and helpful guidance is fine, so long as it's well intentioned and your observations are specific and helpful. But if you make a habit of criticising others, many people will probably try to avoid you.

We all know someone who is hypercritical. That person who always discovers a way to take the mood of a conversation down by finding fault in anything and everything. They make few compliments and offer little praise. Knowing someone like this can be a valuable life lesson as their tiresome mindset clearly demonstrates how *not* to be. Notice how they moan, nit-pick and complain about everything – and then do the opposite. Don't be that person!

Mind your own business

A critical habit becomes even worse when the issue at hand is none of your business. Do you ever hear yourself saying 'I wouldn't do that if I were him' or 'I can't believe she did that' or 'What were they thinking'? If you're troubled about something you can't control or is none of your business, then think twice before interfering or making negative comments about other people's affairs. If you can help people, then show your good intentions by offering assistance, but also have the humility and wisdom to back off and mind your own business when your input is not required.

Remember: Constructive feedback can be a useful tool when used wisely, but incessant criticism is a bad habit. Try to ditch this bad habit and replace it with open-mindedness, kindness and patience. Not everyone will see the world the way you see it. Not everyone will want the same things as you – maybe they have different values. Everyone has their faults, including you, so try to embrace the differences between you and the rest of mankind.

36

LEADERSHIP

Do you see yourself as a leader?

Leadership isn't for everyone, so you may or may not find this chapter useful. However, I recommend giving it a quick read because leadership isn't just about running a business or addressing and motivating a room full of people. It could be as simple as mentoring a colleague, managing an assistant at work, serving on a committee or organising a social event. Whatever the scenario, absorbing and applying the basic principles of leadership can be a character-building and life-enhancing experience.

Qualities of a good leader

Good leaders are endowed with an unassuming confidence that inspires and motivates those around them. Respectful and composed, they're ready to invest their time in developing others, rather than simply to dictate and control. Good leaders encourage teamwork and they have a 'can do' growth mindset, which minimises people's fears about being out of their depth. They're good communicators, they ask questions and they encourage their staff to find their own solutions.

Good leaders define projects and set targets for their team so that everyone is moving in the same direction. People have an irresistible desire to believe in something, and good leaders harness that desire; they offer their team a worthy cause to get behind and throw down a challenge. They attach meaning and importance to their staff's work by giving them a noble motive. For example, an employee would much prefer to see their job as 'making the company website the best in the industry' instead of 'writing software'.

Establish learning habits

Good leaders are continually developing their skills and searching for new knowledge, and they make sure their team does the same. People gain a sense of pride and satisfaction as they progress and acquire new skills, because they're developing into the person they want to be.

Try This: One way of introducing a learning culture within a business is to make books freely accessible via an in-house business library. The effectiveness of this concept can be taken up a notch by starting a book club, whereby team members discuss and exchange ideas from a book they've all read. Most people would like to work for a business in which staff are permanently learning new skills, swapping ideas, developing and bonding as a team.

Team dynamics

Teams that concentrate more on people's strengths are more effective than teams that pay too much attention to people's weaknesses. Weaknesses will need to be addressed from time to time, but when team members are aware of each individual's strengths, the group can organise itself to get the most out of them. Managers also need to monitor team moral and observe how well everyone is collaborating and building strong business relationships.

Positivity

A leader's attitude will spread quickly throughout the team so it's imperative for leaders to stay upbeat, constructive and professional. This means being cheerful, generous, optimistic and enthusiastic, because they know people are happier when positive people are around.

Build Bonds

Managers can also build bonds and boost team moral by enquiring about their staff's personal lives and reminding them of their value in the workplace. In addition to appreciation, successful managers display friendliness, compassion and humility to their staff, and are willing to cultivate a social rapport with each team member.

Autonomy

Good leaders motivate by trusting and having faith in their staff. They delegate responsibility and give people the freedom to make business decisions on behalf of the company. This creates an ethos of trust and encourages staff to step out of their comfort zone. They also make it clear that they're always available to help. The old cliché 'Don't bring me a problem without a solution' doesn't always make sense, because if staff don't talk to you about major issues early enough, they can snowball out of control.

Resistance

Experienced leaders anticipate resistance and don't get discouraged by it; nor do they resist the resistance, because resistors have their own concerns that need to be taken on board. Impatient leaders identify some staff as regular initiators of resistance, and this can exasperate them so much that they start making unilateral decisions without consulting their team at all. Staff then react to being overlooked by resisting even more. Instead, leaders should show respect for people's opinions. They should be sympathetic toward their ideas and needs, and genuinely try to see things from their point of view.

A skilled leader helps their team appreciate the unseen advantages of change, such as the acquisition of new skills, the building of new relationships and other new opportunities that may arise.

Team building

A functioning team is usually much more effective than a collection of individuals working independently, provided team members collaborate efficiently. If staff have widely differing approaches, however, there is potential for friction within the team. For example, some individuals are methodical while others are chaotic, and some employees are highly driven, while others are not. Effective leaders are constantly on high alert for personality clashes within their team and they do their best to nip it in the bud before it gets out of hand.

Honest Appraisals

Research has found that the top 10 per cent of employees are 80 per cent more productive than the average employee and 700 per cent more productive than employees in the bottom decile. Unfortunately, the majority of employees overrate their competence and contribution, so honest staff appraisals are a vital tool in the pursuit of higher standards. Good leaders understand that people are their greatest resource and are fixated on creating and maintaining a high quality team producing top quality work.

They also don't forget to express their gratitude by sending individual letters of thanks to those staff who go that extra mile.

Let go of dead weight

Unfortunately, nothing will satisfy the perpetual agitator and destroyer of harmony. Even the most patient leaders are best advised not to appease these people. For the good of all, their influence needs to be eliminated.

When a business appoints an employee, a contract is signed by both parties. The business pays that employee while the employee executes their duties at an acceptable level. When individuals cannot or will not execute their duties satisfactorily and become dead weight, the business ought not to feel guilty about terminating their contract. High-performing staff recognise that this must be done, and they appreciate a strong leader who doesn't hesitate to act swiftly when removing poor performers. The remaining staff benefit by working in an environment full of hardworking and motivated people.

Feedback

As well as giving thoughtful and honest feedback to their staff, good leaders welcome feedback on their own performance. It might not always be pleasant, but secure leaders understand that they too need a bit of critical feedback to help them develop their managerial skills. They also know that asking for advice, instead of just opinions, encourages staff to put themselves in their shoes which creates a unique bond between employee and manager. Successful leaders also actively seek out help and develop strong relationships with peers and mentors who are in a position to support them in achieving their goals.

Ethical leadership

Ethics are becoming increasingly important to leaders and employees. Staff with ethical managers feel that their work is more meaningful and they themselves are less likely to demonstrate unethical conduct. The requirement for ethical business practice is likely to become the norm as customers and other stakeholders apply more scrutiny to the business world at large.

Remember: Without leaders, it's very difficult to manage large groups of people and set unified goals that enable the group to progress. Good leaders demonstrate integrity, accountability, humility and resilience, and they inspire others to follow their vision.

37

ENERGY

Are you feeling tired? Optimise your energy.

While the brain is just 2 per cent of a person's body weight, it accounts for 20 per cent of the body's energy use, so if our energy levels are low our brain functioning will drop off in equal measure. The six key factors influencing our energy levels are diet, sleep, exercise, mental attitude, chronotype and life balance. The following chapter is dedicated entirely to guidance on sleep, so in this chapter, I will cover the other five major energy influencers.

Eating a balanced diet

There are many sources of information on this subject and a detailed description of what we should and shouldn't eat is beyond the scope of this book. Most dietary advice centres around eating a wide variety of healthy food and drink in the right proportions, in order to achieve a healthy body weight:

- Eat at least five portions of a variety of fruit and vegetables every day
- Base meals on higher fibre starchy foods like potatoes, bread, rice or pasta
- Have some dairy or dairy alternatives (such as soya drinks)
- Eat some beans, pulses, fish, eggs, meat and other protein
- Choose unsaturated oils and spreads, and eat them in small amounts
- Drink plenty of water and other fluids

If you consume foods and drinks that are high in fat, salt and sugar, have these less often and in small amounts. Try to choose a variety of different foods from the food groups listed above to get a wide range of nutrients. In truth many people eat and drink too many calories, including too much saturated fat, sugar and salt, and not enough fruit, vegetables, oily fish or fibre. Set a target body weight range that's both achievable and appropriate for you. In order to stay in that weight range, weigh yourself every week and adjust your eating and exercise habits accordingly.

Exercise

It may seem contradictory that exercise, which makes us feel physically tired, is one of the most essential things we can do to boost our energy and fight fatigue. But it's true. Regular exercise improves energy by:

- Increasing muscle mass
- Increasing the heart's pumping volume
- Reducing body fat
- Lowering fat in the blood such as bad cholesterol
- Improving the body's regulation of blood sugar
- Improving circulation
- Boosting mood and mental capacity

We all know that working out is good for us and some people make exercise a non-negotiable and consistent habit. Other people, on the other hand, are excellent at dreaming up convoluted explanations and justifications to skip their daily work out. Don't be one of them!

Mental attitude

To create and maintain mental energy, you need to develop an upbeat and optimistic mindset. Research shows that high-fliers are more jovial and optimistic than the average person, even though their professional lives are much more hectic. They deliberately focus on the positives and resist negative self-talk, resulting in a happier disposition and higher levels of vitality and drive.

If this describes you, then you are one of the lucky people to whom optimism comes naturally. Most of us, however, regularly experience negative emotions and begin each day with a multitude of difficult situations on our minds. When you feel a little down or overwhelmed, you cannot simply turn on the 'happiness' switch and instantly feel energised. There will always be times when you feel sad, and this is okay. Just remember that these periods will pass.

Try This: One strategy that often helps is to deliberately begin each day with positive intentions and expectations. Pause for one minute each morning to visualise a few things that you're looking forward to during the day ahead. When we anticipate something good happening, the neurotransmitter dopamine is released, resulting in positive feelings. Therefore, by looking forward to a positive event, you get double the happiness – the anticipation of the event and the event itself.

If you need to give yourself a bit of a pep talk, try to recall a period or moment in your life when you were intensely animated and buzzing. Another word one could use to describe these periods is 'flourishing' and they're accompanied by a sense of progress, accomplishment and energy. In business, flourishing workers report high levels of job fulfilment, inspiration, resilience and confidence. They experience less stress and fatigue because their work boosts their energy rather than sapping it. When we're flourishing, we have drive and determination, and we're excited to get out of bed in the morning.

Ask yourself: 'Am I flourishing?' If not, why not? Refer to Chapter 1 on values, Chapter 3 on optimism and Chapter 7 on goals. How can you change things so you can flourish in the future?

Chronotype

Each of us has a unique circadian rhythm that determines our natural energy levels during a typical 24-hour cycle. While we're all different, people tend to fall into one of three main types called chronotypes:

- **Standard:** A feeling of higher energy that peaks in the morning. It then falls off in the afternoon and steadily ramps up again in the evening.
- **Early bird:** The same as standard, but the peak, drop off and ramp up all happen a few hours earlier.
- **Night owl:** Energy peaks at around 9 p.m.

Most of us have the standard chronotype, so our mornings are most likely to be the best time to handle important or difficult tasks that necessitate high levels of analytical brain power. Tasks that demand creative thinking are better left to the late afternoon or early evening, leaving undemanding tasks to be tackled during the low point in the early afternoon. With a bit of trial and error, you should be able to work out your chronotype, but be aware that things change as we get older. Young children and the elderly are largely early birds. Teenagers, on the other hand, tend to be night owls.

Life balance

Many people think that working for long stretches without a break is the only route to maximum productivity. They need to think again! DeskTime, a company specialising in software for tracking employee productivity, did a study of the most productive employees to better understand their work routine. From their data, the most productive people work for 52 minutes and then take a break for 17 minutes. These short periods of work produce great results because they're essentially sprints – intensive, purposeful work sessions that come after a proper rest.

During breaks, it's important to ignore all emails and other work-related business during the time off. Socialising is a proven stress reducer, as is going for a quick walk outside or eating a healthy snack.

According to the Mental Health Foundation, the pressure of an increasingly demanding work culture is one of the biggest challenges to society's mental health. A healthy work-life balance will mean different things to us all. It's not so much about splitting your life 50/50 between work and leisure, but making sure you feel fulfilled and content in both areas of your life. A healthy balance might look like:

- Meeting your deadlines at work while still having time for your family, friends and hobbies
- Having enough time to sleep properly and eat well

- Not worrying about work when you're at home

Try This: Pause. Ask yourself: what's currently causing me stress or unhappiness? How is that affecting my work and personal life? What am I prioritising? What am I losing out on? What are my alternatives? Each week, decide where your focus is needed and prioritise your energy accordingly. Identify the least effective and most energy-sapping activities in your life and try to remove or reduce them.

38

SLEEP

Do you get enough sleep?

Over the past few decades, both sleep quality and quantity have declined, with many people regularly getting poor sleep. This is a worrying trend because sleep plays a key role in our health and has the same importance as exercise and diet. Poor sleep has a negative effect on our hormones and brain function, it can cause us to gain weight and it can increase our susceptibility to disease. If we want to optimise our health, mood or weight, then getting a good night's sleep is one of the most important things we can do.

Exercise

Exercise is one of the best ways to improve your sleep. One study in older adults revealed that exercise nearly halved the amount of time it took to fall asleep and provided an average of 41 more minutes of sleep per night. In people with severe insomnia, exercise offered more benefits than most drugs. Exercise reduced the time to fall asleep by 55 per cent, reduced total night wakefulness by 30 per cent and reduced anxiety by 15 per cent, while increasing total sleep time by 18 per cent.

While daily exercise is clearly helpful, don't work out late in the day. Doing so can cause sleep problems due to the stimulatory effects of increased alertness and the excessive release of hormones such as epinephrine and adrenaline.

The circadian rhythm

As I mention in Chapter 37, the body has a biological timekeeping clock known as the circadian rhythm which influences the brain, body and hormones. The circadian rhythm helps us stay awake and informs our body when it's time to sleep. The following all affect your circadian rhythm, and thus your ability to sleep:

- **Daytime light:** Exposure to natural sunlight or bright light during the day helps keep the circadian rhythm healthy, improving both sleep quality and duration. Research on people with insomnia found that daytime bright light exposure improved sleep quality and reduced the time it took to fall asleep by 83 per cent. While most of this research has been done on people with severe sleep issues, daily light exposure will most likely help everyone. Where possible, exercise outside, but if exposure to natural light isn't always practical, consider investing in a specialist artificial bright light.

- **Night-time light:** Exposure to light at night has the opposite effect to daytime light exposure because it tricks the brain into thinking it's still daytime by reducing hormones like melatonin, which helps us relax into a deep sleep. Exposure to blue light from smartphones and computers is particularly bad, so keep away from these screens late at night. If this is impractical, try wearing glasses that block blue light or download an app to block blue light on your computer or smartphone. Also, turn off any bright lights two hours before bedtime.

- **Caffeine:** This stimulates the nervous system, and consuming it late in the day may stop the body naturally relaxing at night. In one study, consuming caffeine up to six hours before bed significantly worsened sleep quality, so if you do crave a cup of coffee in the late afternoon or evening, drink decaffeinated instead.

- **Alcohol:** This causes or increases the symptoms of sleep apnoea (see the next section), snoring and disrupted sleep patterns. It also alters night-time melatonin production. A study revealed that alcohol consumption at night decreased the natural night-time elevations in human growth hormone (HGH), which plays a role in the circadian rhythm and other key functions.

- **Late-night eating:** This can negatively impact the natural release of HGH and melatonin, and so reduce sleep quality.

- **Sleep schedule:** The circadian rhythm operates on a set loop, usually aligned with sunrise and sunset, so maintaining consistency of bedtime and waking time helps with long-term sleep quality. Inconsistent sleep patterns can alter your circadian rhythm and interfere with your levels of melatonin. Short, regular power naps of 30 minutes or less can be beneficial to some, but taking long or irregular naps during the day often has a negative effect on our sleep because these naps confuse our internal clock.

Medical issues that disturb sleep

Nocturia is the medical term for excessive urination during the night. It can adversely affect sleep quality, and so if you suffer from nocturia it's well worth consulting a medical professional. Your doctor will advise you on some conservative methods that may help to improve your symptoms, and if this doesn't help, you may be offered medication depending on the cause of your condition. Drinking large amounts of liquids before bed can lead to similar symptoms, so it's wise to reduce your fluid intake in the late evening.

Another common medical problem is sleep apnoea, which causes inconsistent and interrupted breathing. One study claimed that 24 per cent of men and 9 per cent of women have sleep apnoea.

Other common medically diagnosed issues include sleep movement disorders and circadian rhythm sleep/wake disorders, which are common in shift workers. If you've always struggled with sleep, consult your doctor.

Supplements

Melatonin supplements are a popular sleep aid and are often used to treat insomnia. In one study, 2 milligrams of melatonin before bed improved sleep quality and energy the next day and helped people fall asleep faster, with little or no withdrawal effects. Start with a low dose (1 milligram) to assess your tolerance and then increase it slowly as needed. Since melatonin can alter brain chemistry, check with a medical professional before use.

Other supplements such as **ginkgo biloba, glycine, valerian root, magnesium, L-theanine and lavender** have been shown to induce relaxation and help with sleep. While there's no magic formula, some of these supplements may be useful when combined with other sleeping strategies.

Sleeping pills

Most research suggests that sleeping pills only slightly reduce the time taken to go to sleep and slightly improve the length of time spent sleeping. The net benefit is therefore marginal. If you're considering taking sleeping pills, consult with you doctor first and together you can make a treatment plan. Sleeping pills were originally designed for temporary use at times of our lives when we really need them, so if you use them, use them sparingly.

A comfortable bedroom

Your bedroom environment, especially temperature, noise, light and mattress quality, are very important factors. A room temperature of 20°C seems to be comfortable for most people, but this will depend on personal preference. Try to minimise external noise, external light and artificial lights from devices and clocks.

What about your mattress? One study looked at the benefits of a new, good-quality mattress for 28 days and found that it reduced back pain by 57 per cent, shoulder pain by 60 per cent and back stiffness by 59 per cent, and improved sleep quality by 60 per cent. Other studies have shown that new bedding can enhance sleep. Make your bedroom a comfortable, quiet, relaxing, clean and enjoyable place.

Wind-down routine

Many people have a pre-sleep routine that helps them wind down. Strategies worth a try include:

- Listening to chilled music
- Reading a book
- Taking a hot bath

- Meditating
- Mindfulness techniques (see Chapter 45)

Remember: Sleep is indispensable! It lets your body and brain recharge, leaving you rested, reinvigorated and alert when you wake. It also helps the body remain healthy and fend off sickness. Inadequate sleep brings inadequate brain functioning, impairing your abilities to focus, concentrate and store memories. Make it a priority to get a good night's sleep.

39

WORRY

Do you worry too much?

Have you ever had a great idea but then went off it because you worried too much about the potential pitfalls? Do you struggle to fall asleep because you're plagued with worry about anxious thoughts? Many people worry about all manner of things, but as mentioned in Chapter 14, only 10 per cent of what we worry about actually happens. So if most of our worries are entirely speculative, why do we worry so much?

Why worry?

Worrying occurs when we think about hypothetical problems. We experience stress triggered solely by our imagination, and because humans have such vivid imaginations our brains get caught up in all sorts of daunting scenarios.

If you only remember one thing from this chapter, remember this; worry is a perpetual liar! It tells you that you're not good enough. It tells you that people are appraising or judging you. It gives you an utterly misleading assessment of your life and drains your energy as you contemplate stressful, yet entirely fictional scenarios. When the brain is worried or anxious on a consistent basis, the neural pathways become more established and this becomes the default setting.

But the fact is, excess worrying does little to help us and in later life we're likely to regret it. Dr Karl Pillemer, a Professor of Human Development at Cornell University, spent nearly a decade interviewing 1,500 senior citizens. When asked about their major regrets, nearly every one of them said they wished they hadn't spent so much of their life worrying.

So if you worry too much, what can you do about it? Here are a few strategies we can employ that might help us worry a little less.

Redirect your attention

We can steer our attention away from the things that activate worry and anxiety by participating in activities such as sport, exercise, hobbies, meditation and sex. Just taking a long walk can be very helpful. The part of the brain that controls anxiety – the amygdala – can only do one thing at a time and walking has been shown to shut it down a little. It's also highly therapeutic to look around and actively notice everything around you, so it's better to walk in places where the scenery captures your interest.

Analysing your worries

While distraction can be useful, I strongly recommend tackling worries head on. If 90 per cent of worries are unsubstantiated, then we need to question them, and the best way to do this is to write them down.

Try This: Follow this process to analyse your worries:

- **Write down your worries in a list.**
- **Read what you've written out loud and question each worry.**
  - Is there any faulty logic hiding within it?
  - Is the probability of it actually happening extremely low? Can you measure this probability in numbers? If so, what are the numbers?
  - What do you think another reasonable person might think about it?
  - What would a starving child in Africa think about it?
  - What would a terminally ill cancer patient think about it?

These questions and their answers should help you to bring context and perspective to your worries.

- **For each of your worries, ask: 'Do I have any control over this?'** Usually, our worries are futile because they concern things out of our control. For example, if your upcoming flight crashes, you'll have had no control over it. (If this thought still makes you uncomfortable, go and analyse the statistics because air travel is one of the safest forms of travel there is.)

- **If you can control any of the issues, write a list of things you can do to avoid the worrying event and then take action.** Taking action is useful for two reasons: firstly, taking action is positive and proactive whereas worrying is passive and reactive, and secondly, your actions might improve your life circumstances.

When you've been through this process a few times, you might find it useful to look for any repeating themes to your worrying. Do certain people make you worried? Or a specific place or type of place? Hopefully, analysing your worries will remove a few from your worry list, or at least reduce their intensity.

Thought experiment: The worst happens

Try This: For a given worry, follow these steps:

- **Imagine that it actually will happen and write down the consequences.** This isn't for the faint-hearted and I certainly wouldn't advocate imagining the death of a loved one. If something is worrying you, however, you do need to challenge those worries, so begin by visualising things like your business failing, your partner leaving or failing that exam.

- **Write down all the actions you could take in the event of this happening.** Worrying often occurs when we refuse to come to terms with the worst potential consequence, so it helps to firstly accept it. The very process of accepting that a particular worry could come true lessens its power over you. The process of predicting what you would do diminishes its power even more.

- **Write a list of things you could do to ensure the worrying outcome doesn't happen.** This is similar to Step 4 in the preceding section, 'Analysing your worries'.

This process of planning and problem-solving will put you more on the front foot and you'll be operating in a more positive, proactive mode. When you accept and then challenge your worries in the methodical way described above, they will become easier to deal with and less intense.

Thought experiment: Time Perspective

Simply ask yourself this question: 'Will I care about this in 12 months?' Whatever the problem or worry you have now, in all likelihood you probably won't care too much in 12 months' time. Maybe even six months' time? By then, it will be a minor bump in the road that's long gone.

Turn to Chapter 28 for more on perspective.

Acceptance

If you regularly make mountains out of molehills, try instead to make molehills out of mountains by viewing your worries and problems as an expected part of living a balanced life. Your happiness isn't dependent on getting rid of all your problems, but on changing your approach to them. Many problems do need to be addressed, so just treat them like any other task and deal with them. However, we do create worries and problems of our own, for example by being an unrealistic perfectionist, or by being greedy, envious, careless, lazy or impatient.

Whatever strategies we use, we'll never be able to stop worrying completely, so the best strategy of all is to accept life, as it is, with all its imperfections. And that means accepting these imperfections without having to understand, influence or control them. It's perfectly fine to say, 'I don't understand, I don't have all the answers, I don't know for sure what will happen in the future'.

Things just happen. That's it. They do not necessarily happen for a reason. There isn't any structured significance to what happens to us other than the interpretations we make up in our heads.

We sometimes feel we should be flawless, and we sometimes forget that mistakes are actually okay and are part of the learning process.

Look at your life choices as chances to experiment and live your life in new ways. New roads lead to new adventures and once you've realised that you can deal with the ups and downs, you will allow yourself to take more chances and to open yourself up to more possibilities.

Remember: Our lives will always include worries and problems, and the techniques in this chapter will give hopefully provide you with a few coping mechanisms. Worrying too much about future situations or achievements can prevent you from being happy right now, and in any given moment there are usually more things to be grateful for than to be anxious about.

If every person on the planet threw all of their problems and worries on one giant pile for redistribution, we'd probably grab ours back! You can spend so much of your energy worrying about little things that you completely forget about the wonder and marvel of life. If you keep your cool and stay open to possibilities, all will be well.

40

PEER PRESSURE

Do you care what other people think?

How many of your worries are connected to concern about other people's opinions? Have you ever tried to impress somebody by behaving in a different way? Maybe to advance your career or curry favour or fit in? Do you think about how family, friends and colleagues evaluate your choices? Do you get a sense of self-worth from winning the positive opinion of others? If we're being totally honest, most of us would probably answer yes to one or more of these questions because our perception of other people's opinions really matters. It acts as a powerful motive for self-evaluation.

Very young children are virtually carefree and unconcerned about what other people think of them, but as they grow older they begin to do what others expect them to do. Adolescents are particularly influenced by the opinions of their friends, especially on social media where they try hard to come over as cool, daring and successful. Even as adults, when we're uncertain of what to do we often look for guidance from those around us. We look at what everyone else is doing before we decide for ourselves. This predisposition is especially strong when these people are like us.

Accept the person in the mirror

While there are many products and treatments designed to make us thinner, better looking and more youthful, many of us still feel bad about our looks. No one worries about our looks but us, so why are we all so apprehensive about it?

Standards of beauty, as portrayed by images in the media, have risen to the point where many people look at these images and think they're just not good enough. We also worry about ageing, but ironically older people hardly ever worry about ageing! Maturity and wisdom help old people understand that stressing about their looks doesn't make them look younger, it just makes them feel bad. So why bother?

The best way to feel good about your weight, your looks or your age is to acknowledge and embrace them. You're not going to transform the media's definition of desirability, but you can change yours. For example, consider the people you love and cherish. Do you often think about their physical flaws? Probably not, but even when you do it makes little difference because you love them. And that is far more important in the grand scheme of things.

Make your self-esteem dependent on your inner, not outer beauty. Focus on what you like about your persona; your talents, personality, opinions and attitude. Remember, these things won't fade with age, they'll always be with you, so be kinder to yourself and love yourself the way you are.

Live for you, not others

Take a little time to pause and reflect on the following questions:

- Why do you choose to remain in your current job?
- Why do you live where you live?
- Do you enjoy how you spend your leisure time?
- Is there anything that you do or don't do because of what a specific person or group of people might think?

In each of these cases, do your deepest desires enter the equation? Many of us concern ourselves with what people think, to the point that we're scared to go after our true goals. This is sad because attempting to get other people's approval means surrendering control of our own destiny: we feel we have to adapt to their definition of success.

If you learn one thing from this chapter, make it this: you're under no obligation to live your life according to the expectations of other people. There will obviously be occasions where you need to do the right thing for your family or employer, but your opinion should always be respected and taken into consideration.

Some external judgements will contain a small piece of truth and will serve to help you grow, but be careful not to confuse these opinions with those motivated by malice or jealousy. We can't prevent other people from being judgemental, and no matter how hard you try some individuals will always find fault in what you do. For example, there'll always be negative attitudes about those who are successful or doing something different. This kind of criticism is their issue and not yours, so ignore it. (For more on handling criticism, see Chapter 35.)

Don't try to mind-read people either – what other people think of you is out of your control, and you might be misjudging the situation anyway. In truth, most of the time other people don't really care that much about you, your appearance or your life choices anyway, so don't overthink or overdramatise these judgements.

Be yourself

If someone says to you something like 'you must be mad doing/not doing ABC', feel free to retort with something like: 'I might be mad in your world, but I don't live in your world, I live in my world, and doing ABC is fine with me'. The most significant bond you have isn't with anybody else – it's with yourself. You don't need to put on an act to impress someone else; your individuality is what will attract people to you – the right people.

Don't bend to pressure: say 'no'

Attempting to be all things to everyone prevents you from being your authentic self, so stop doing things you don't want to do by saying a firm but polite 'no'. If you repeatedly do things you're not keen on, you'll end up resenting the people asking you to do these things, and if they sense you're unhappy, they'll feel guilty for asking you do something you don't want to do. This is clearly a lose-lose situation.

Choose your friends wisely

The people you surround yourself with have a big impact on your own attitude and demeanour. For example, you are 15 per cent more likely to be happy yourself if you surround yourself with happy people. So when a friend (or a partner) doesn't support you, or holds you back, or doesn't share your positivity, perhaps it's time to rethink the relationship.

Surround yourself with encouraging and supportive people – people you look up to, people who have similar passions, and people you love and trust. Seek out those who want you to do well, and make sure you give something back to them as well as receiving. As you build your social circle, explore new groups, places and communities where you can meet like-minded people from all walks of life.

Be humble, be human, be vulnerable, be true, be you!

41

ANGER

Does anger work for you or against you?

It's perfectly normal to get angry – it's a natural emotion. We do need to be careful with it, however, because anger characterises an attitude of superiority, self-entitlement, criticism and blame. It might feel like a rational reaction to a situation, but it is often irrational, overdramatised and way out of proportion with the issue at hand.

The 'ugly' emotion

We all know that bottling up anger inside creates internal tension that can be downright draining, yet we often keep a lid on our anger because we think it's wrong to let it out – it's supposedly an 'ugly' emotion. When anger is suppressed, however, it might build and build, and eventually erupt in the form of rage, yelling or physical aggression. Unresolved or continuous anger is exhausting and can lead to a weakened immune system, high blood pressure and migraines.

Anger is a formidable force of nature that, if unchecked, will end up harming ourselves and the people around us. During violent bursts of anger, we say and do things we wouldn't ordinarily do. It's hard to feel relaxed in the company of highly strung people who are disposed to furious bouts of anger, as they might explode at any minute.

We all get angry from time to time, but different people deal with their anger in different ways. Some people might respond to a given situation with mild irritation, whereas other people might respond with violent rage. The former response is clearly a better outcome than the latter, so how do we acknowledge, deal with, and express our anger in beneficial and constructive ways?

Pause!

Anger is an emotion that often hits us suddenly like a five-metre-high wave crushing onto a beach. If our anger acts with the same force as this wave at its breaking point, then woe betide anyone that gets in its way. If, however, we wait for a few seconds and allow our anger to dissipate, we will be calmer, just like the wave's backwash, gentle trickling back into the ocean. This metaphor might sound simplistic, but it is quite similar to the perennial 'calming' technique of taking a few deep breaths while counting to 10.

Pausing in this way won't right any wrongs, but it will help take the heat out of the situation and give us time to calm down and think more carefully about what we would like to say. If we stay cool our words will carry more weight, our opinions will be taken more seriously, and we are more likely to get what we want out of the situation.

Find the emotion behind the anger

We often use anger to hide behind emotions such as hurt, irritation, fear or shame. So there's little point in simply telling someone 'I'm angry with you' without identifying exactly why you're angry. They'll probably feel your anger is unwarranted and won't understand what's really happening. It's much more effective to say 'It hurt me when you snubbed me yesterday' or 'I'm afraid you don't value me anymore'.

Try This: Before you get too angry with someone, think carefully about your true feelings. Then tell the person the true source of your anger in a non-confrontational way. You may say something like this:

'I love you and I appreciate that you continually give me support when I want and need it the most. But I do find it upsetting when you don't have time for me. I'm fearful that you're not interested in me anymore. Maybe we should spend more time together in the evenings? What do you think?'

Choose not to argue

We live in a world full of wonderful people, but there's always going to be somebody who'll get angry and want to argue with you. Remember that you don't have to match your opponent blow for blow – it takes two parties to fight, and even if someone provokes you, an argument can only take place if you get drawn into it. It's the other person's anger that's talking, not yours, so if you don't want to argue, simply answer calmly: 'You're obviously very angry about this.' This type of comment implies that you've noticed their anger but aren't necessarily going to get angry yourself. Trying to take the intensity out of situations like this doesn't mean you have to be submissive. Just put your point across in a tone of voice that's cool, composed and assertive.

For more on conflict and arguing, see Chapter 42.

Breathe!

Try This: When your anger is suddenly about to explode, you breathe more quickly, you go red, you tense up and your heart races. As soon as you realise this could be happening, take 10 deep breaths and tell yourself that this sensation of rage will soon be over. Try to distract yourself by thinking about something completely unrelated to what is making you angry. Maybe think about what you'll be having for dinner? Or pick up a random object in your vicinity and inspect it in detail. This, and the slow breathing, should help you to calm down. Then, when you feel a little calmer, revisit the situation making you angry. Can you think of anything good about it? For example, if you've missed a flight, you could think about it as an opportunity to catch up on some reading.

Let go

The cause of most anger emanates from our wish to control everything and our reluctance to embrace life when it doesn't deliver what we expect. But life isn't always the way we'd like it to be – it is what it is. When we accept and enjoy life as it is, we're free of the burden of having to have everything done in a certain way. When you approach each day with this attitude and don't expect everything to go exactly as planned, you'll soon notice things falling into place with much less fuss and life will be much more pleasurable. You'll discover that many of the things that have always angered you will cease to be an issue. Your perspective changes. This is a wonderful way to live.

Slow down

When our lives become hectic and busy with too many things to do, it feels practical to continually push ourselves. We rush through breakfast, rush to work, rush through our working day trying to fit everything in, and then we rush home again. It's so easy to get irritated and angry when we live our lives on the edge like this.

Try taking your time and slowing down a little rather than hurrying everywhere. When driving, for example, allow a little extra time and drive slowly. Take the time to notice things as you pass them by and enjoy the serenity of not rushing. Employ a similar strategy and slow down other activities in your life. You'll find you get less angry the more you embrace a more tranquil state of mind.

Sleep and exercise

Sleep deprivation increases irritability, and you'll view the world more clearly and positively with a good night's sleep under your belt. Regular exercise is another excellent way to make yourself feel more cheerful and calm.

Practise gratitude

People often feel angry because they're not getting what they want from a relationship, a job or life generally. If we change our perspective and focus on the things we do have and fully appreciate them, this gratitude will help us feel better about our life generally, and hopefully a little less angry.

Try This: Begin every day by making a mental or written list of some of the things you're grateful for: the building you live in, the food in the fridge or the beautiful weather outside. For more on gratitude, see Chapter 52.

Make peace with the past

Anger can be the result of painful memories. Maybe a school bully used to mock you in front of everyone, and because of that you now get angry when anyone teases you, even if it's a bit of harmless fun. You feel the anger in the present because you've suppressed all the anger and vengeance you feel against that bully in the past, and you become confused and neurotic because you don't realise where your anger is coming from.

It's essential to address hurtful events from your past and tackle them head on. Begin by acknowledging to yourself that certain incidents from the past still upset you. Then find someone you can talk to about them – maybe a trained counsellor or a wise friend. These conversations will bring into play another person's viewpoint and will hopefully throw up some sound advice. The goal is to put these memories into perspective, make peace with them and move on.

Remember: Your life will never be flawless so work on accepting what life has to offer with a calm demeanour. Follow the guidance of the Serenity Prayer: change the things that can be changed, acknowledge and accept those that can't, and have the wisdom to know the difference.

42

CONFLICT

Do you need to be right all the time? Learn to argue constructively.

Admitting we're wrong provides a huge threat to our ego so it often responds to this threat by arguing – arguing with the sole intention of winning. Our ego doesn't want to learn new things or observe the world through a different lens; it just wants to win. When two people engage in an ego dominated conflict, the outcome is usually bad: both sides stick with their original stance and they refuse to listen to, let alone learn from, the other side's point of view. Constructive interaction therefore becomes impossible.

That said, it's equally as unhealthy to avoid conflict completely and allow issues to build up. If you keep them suppressed over weeks or months, they'll eventually explode like a volcano. It's much better to deal with them as they arise or dismiss them completely.

Pick your battles wisely

Some of us argue over every trivial thing. There's so much irritation and anger bound up in this behaviour that we lose sight of what's really important. Picking your battles wisely involves choosing between letting something go or making an issue out of it. The choice is informed by realising what really matters and what doesn't. For example, showing forgiveness and empathy to your child might be more important than arguing over a dropped glass of milk. Is it critical that you prove that you're right and the other person is wrong? If you pick your battles wisely, you'll be more successful at dealing with the battles that really matter.

Have a goal

If a disagreement or argument is unavoidable, always be mindful of what you're trying to achieve. Ask yourself, 'What is my aim here?' Never argue for the sake of it; only do it when there's a clear goal.

Don't score points

Don't follow the usual pattern of just trying to score points so you can win. This provokes the other person to raise their protective shield and turn the conflict into a war of words. If the other person is intent on scoring points or is trying to demean or insult you, try your best to stay calm. The simple act of pausing to think before speaking will help you stay calm and diffuse the situation.

Listen

When some people argue, they are prepared to use any weapon they can to get their adversary to back down or concede defeat. If this force is met with an equal and opposite resisting force, the argument rapidly escalates into a shouting match, with little chance of resolution. Instead, try a far more effective tactic: listening. When you listen, the other person feels heard and in return, they're more likely to listen to what you have to say. Here are some tips for constructive listening in the midst of a disagreement:

- Listen carefully without coming back with your own arguments.
- Ask questions. Try to fully understand their point of view.
- Make compassion and respect for other people a higher priority than winning; attempt to see the matter from their side.

If you continually interrupt and counter with your own arguments, you're likely to make the other person more resolute, self-justifying and dogmatic. When they feel heard, they'll appreciate you and your opinion far more.

Be prepared to be wrong

If you're wrong, admit it emphatically. Admitting mistakes can be very difficult for our ego and self-image, but it's tremendously important for sustaining relationships and personal growth. We learn an awful lot from our mistakes, so if we don't acknowledge them, we're unlikely to better ourselves. We end up being that person who is both ignorant and arrogant; the one who is 'always right'. Also, people who never admit their mistakes tend to store up subconscious feelings of guilt and shame which can turn into anxiety and depression. Admitting mistakes demonstrates to others that you are considerate and compassionate, and capable of being honest and objective about yourself. People will like you for it.

Conflict avoidance isn't the answer

Many people progress through life trying to avoid conflict. They're natural people pleasers who are more worried about upsetting people than having their opinions heard. If this is you, there's a high probability that you're quite popular and easy to get along with, and that's okay up to a certain point.

If you continually avoid all differences of opinion, you're placing your true feelings at the back of the queue. This will render you incapable of honest communication with other people and all that bottled up frustration you hold inside you will have a negative effect on your mental health. It's not easy, but each day take a few tiny steps toward speaking up for yourself. Make this a habit.

Difficult conversations

So what is the best way to approach conflict? On those occasions when you need to start a conversation that's likely to lead to a disagreement, follow these guidelines:

- **Start in a non-confrontational way.** Don't blame the other person for the problem. Be mindful that this person may not know what's most important to you and have the humility to realise that your preferences are not always the right preferences.

- **Be careful not to make generalisations.** Accusations like 'You never tidy the kitchen', 'You're lazy' and 'You're never on time' aren't helpful. Instead, say something like 'I see that the kitchen needs tidying, it would mean a lot if you could help me get it clean and tidy'.

- **Don't be too critical.** For example, rather than saying 'The other staff work much harder than you – I'm beginning to think you're slacking off', it would be better to say, 'I want to thank you for helping me clear out the storeroom the other day; you did a great job. I'd like to talk to you about helping me out more with sales data and reporting. The sales team are very busy out there and they need as much assistance as they can get. If you could do that for the team, we would all be forever grateful.'

- **Be ready with the solution.** Or even better, ask the person to brainstorm with you what the solution might be.

Obviously, this kind of dialogue takes a little thought and preparation, so delicate conversations of this nature might need to be rehearsed in advance. Try not to worry or speculate too much about it, because in all likelihood it'll be much easier than you had expected.

Misunderstandings

No matter how much we try to be constructive and caring, we will occasionally hurt someone's feelings. If this happens, begin by asking a few questions so you can better understand their position and hopefully identify why the misunderstanding has occurred. At this stage, try not to allocate blame or go on the defensive. It could have been that your exact choice of words didn't come out as you'd planned or that your tone of voice sounded different than you'd intended. If you make the effort to understand how and why the misunderstanding happened, you'll better understand how to change your approach next time.

Take a time out

One way to take the heat out of a situation is to ask for a time out. If agreed by both parties, put some physical distance between yourself and the situation. This will give everyone time to think. Go somewhere quiet and private and take a few deep breaths. This will enable you to think more clearly and manage your anger before it gets out of control.

Create a level playing field

If we feel attacked, we release adrenaline which in turn causes our emotions to overrule rational and logical thinking. We may get furious and try to hammer our opinion across by raising our voice and relentlessly interjecting before other people have chance to finish what they're saying. In order to avoid this, all parties need to agree that voices are not to be raised and everyone should be allowed to speak without interruption. With these ground rules established, also consider the following:

- **Establishing a feeling of mutual respect:** To build respect, you need to be mindful of how you speak to people. For example, if you need to talk to a male employee about tardiness, you could firstly stress that you're happy with most aspects of his work and then say that the only problem is that he is very slow at responding to emails and voice messages.

- **Identifying a shared purpose:** People need to feel that both sides are attempting to find a solution, so it's important to try to establish what this solution might look like as early as possible in the dialogue.

Encourage the other person to speak freely and then paraphrase back to them your understanding of what they're saying. This will make them feel that you understand their position and that their honesty is appreciated. It will also slow you down enough to take the heat out of your responses.

Look for the big picture

A source of many arguments is our lack of understanding of other people's behaviour. From time to time we all do weird things, so try to cast a less critical eye on the unconventional actions of others. Try to see the bigger picture; this might help you discover what factors are influencing their behaviour. This type of compassionate thinking will help curb your criticism and replace it with empathy.

Be the one to offer the olive branch

It's all too easy to cling on to anger arising from long out-of-date altercations. We doggedly wait for the other party to apologise because we believe we're right and they were wrong. Is our anger more important than our relationships? Probably not. So if someone has the maturity to break the cycle and offer an olive branch, everyone wins. If we hold on to our anger and stubbornly stick to our position, everyone loses. Initiating a reconciliation doesn't mean you're wrong. It means you've made a valuable contribution toward building a more caring, harmonious world.

Remember: Those who are the most comfortable with conflict are those who expect it, accept it and treat it as a positive part of communication.

43

PATIENCE

Be a little more patient.

We all know what impatience is. We feel impatient when something takes longer than we think it should take, or longer than we had expected it to take. My particular bugbear is a long or a slow-moving queue – it drives me nuts and I often get uptight and frustrated when I really should know better. Also, the fast pace of technology has improved the speed and efficiency at which we access all sorts of products and services, which fuels our collective impatience even more when something goes wrong.

Those who develop high levels of patience seem to glide through life effortlessly – they are at ease with the world. The more patient people become, the more tolerant and open-minded they are of what life throws at them, rather than demanding that their lives run precisely how they'd planned. Patient people find a way to be receptive to the current situation, even when it's worse than they'd expected. Being a little more patient is probably a worthy target for all of us.

Try This: Patience is not the ability to wait, but how you act while you are waiting, so try the following ideas for developing your patience. With a little more tolerance you'll start to enjoy many of life's curveballs that once irritated you.

- **Slow down and simplify.** Tight schedules, multitasking and being too busy often lead to impatience. Streamline your workload and allow more time for journeys and important tasks.

- **How does impatience feel to you?** What effect does it have on your body and where do you feel it? Is it in your stomach? Your shoulders? Your chest? Do you get sweaty palms? When you identify the physical feelings associated with impatience, it actually diminishes its intensity.

- **Identify triggers that make you impatient.** Make a list. When you notice that you're getting impatient, ask, 'What exactly is making me impatient right now?' Think about your triggers and their underlying causes. Identify any patterns and consider how you can avoid being impatient in the future.

- **Take deep breaths before your impatience spirals out of control.** Calm yourself down with slow, deep breaths and tell yourself, 'It is what it is'.

- **Distract yourself.** Is there any other activity you can engage in while you're waiting? This will make your waiting time go faster and you'll feel better because at least you can use the time productively. Use of a mobile device is a popular choice.

- **Be positive.** If it's other people making you impatient, look for the good in them, especially the young and old. Instead of getting irritated, remind yourself how blessed you are to have wonderful kids or thriving, healthy parents or grandparents.

- **Keep trying.** When we actively work on our patience, we get better at it, so persevere even if it doesn't work every time.

Let's put these ideas into a real-life example. Consider my dread of queuing. Picture the scene as I walk into an airport and the check-in queue is four times what I expect it to be – my heart sinks! I know this is one of my impatience triggers, so after a few deep breaths, my internal dialogue could go along the following lines: 'I can't change the size of this queue, nor can I make it move any quicker, so I need to make a real effort to be patient. For the next 40 minutes, I'm going to do everything in my power to stay calm. Now, what can I distract myself with?'

Remember: Things won't always go your way, but with patience you'll soon understand that seemingly negative experiences can sometimes become positive experiences. Give it a try!

44

STRESS

Is stress your friend or your enemy?

If your boss approached your desk one morning and praised your work ethic, and then told you to go home and take the rest of the day off, would you do it? Would you go home or would you be too worried about any urgent matters that need your attention?

Self-esteem is closely related to factors like life experience, contentment, self-assurance, relationships, health, job performance and career progression. Unfortunately, many of us attach far too much importance to the last two items on this list: to the detriment of recreation, relaxation and our physical and mental health. Our career goals are so set in stone that we don't allow ourselves to take breaks and have fun.

Workaholics always have a mountain of unfinished work to do. They work excessively hard and long hours, taking very few breaks for rest and relaxation. Holidays, special treats and other fun things are set aside until some unspecified date in the future. If they push themselves to exhaustion, then both their work and well-being will suffer. If they then throw a crisis into the melting pot, cracks begin to appear, and they may even end up having a nervous breakdown.

The perils of too much stress

A frenzied lifestyle saps a lot of energy and can remove the creativity, fun and motivation from our day-to-day living. We barely have time to think; to concentrate; to innovate. Our lives are sometimes so crammed with tasks, errands and obligations, it's very difficult to unwind. We become obsessed with crossing things off our to-do list and this 'hurry sickness' is accompanied by an undercurrent of stress from worrying about all the things we still have to do. And unfortunately, new technology has become part of the problem, not part of the solution.

Worse still, life's stressors overload the body with stress hormones, causing illness and accelerated ageing. Chronic stress occurs when the long-term activation of cortisol and other stress hormones disrupts almost all the bodies processes. This puts us at increased risk of many health problems, including:

- Anxiety
- Depression
- Digestive problems
- Headaches

- Muscle tension and pain
- Heart disease & heart attack
- High blood pressure
- Stroke
- Sleep problems
- Weight gain
- Memory and concentration impairment

Chronic stress usually works quietly behind the scenes without our knowledge, but the effects on our body can be life threatening – that's why stress is sometimes referred to as 'The silent killer'. Keeping your stress under control is therefore crucial.

The importance of rest and fun

Be sure to pay regular attention to the needs of your mind and body. If you think you have too much to do and not enough time to do it in, it might be time to stop for a minute and re-examine what's important, as opposed to what's urgent. And including sufficient downtime *is* important.

Successful people know when to slow down and they appreciate the importance of work breaks and recreation to help them relax and reinvigorate, so they can be dynamic and industrious when they get back to work. This might take the form of games, hobbies, sport, travel, outdoor pursuits, reading or simply watching TV, all of which help clear the mind and reduce stress levels.

Positive stress

Positive stress, otherwise known as good stress or eustress, is the type of stress we feel when we attempt something out of our comfort zone, such as public speaking or rock climbing. If successful, we feel elated, motivated, inspired and we give our self-esteem a huge lift. Eustress helps us become stronger, so we can tackle upcoming challenges with more confidence. The key is to challenge yourself without going too far and draining all your energy reserves.

The ideal amount of stress varies from person to person, but if the stress level is too low we're likely to be unchallenged and uninterested, and because of their elevated levels of testosterone, men typically need more positive stress than women. Everyone's testosterone production lessens as we get older, so it follows that the amount of positive stress needed for optimum performance lessens with age.

Time to de-stress

Many people put off rest and recreation until all the items on their to-do list have been crossed off. But to-do lists are rarely completed, so it's important to deliberately schedule some peaceful 'me time' every day. It's calming and revitalising to be alone and take some time to reflect, read or simply do nothing. It's a vital respite from the busyness that permeates most of the day.

Try This: Take a one-minute 'tranquillity break' a few times a day, whenever you have a moment to yourself. Empty your mind and take five slow, deep breaths and enjoy the feeling of tranquillity that takes over your body. These short tranquillity breaks serve as a gentle introduction to the process of meditation and many people go on to having longer sessions.

Remember: Being under pressure is a normal part of life. It can help you take action, feel more energised and get results. But if you become overwhelmed by stress, these feelings could start to be a problem for your physical and mental health. If you regularly give your brain a rest, it will stay fresh, inventive and calm. You'll be less worrisome and you'll find it easier to concentrate on achieving your goals.

45

MINDFULNESS

Relax, breathe and enjoy the moment.

Mindfulness has become a common self-improvement catchword, but what is it exactly? Unfortunately, there's no easy answer to that question because mindfulness means different things to different people, but I'll do my best to point you in the right direction.

By far the most readable and practical book I've read on the subject is The Power of Now by Eckhart Tolle. I strongly advise you to read the book, or listen to the audio version, which is read by Eckhart himself, with his wonderfully calm and mesmeric voice.

What is mindfulness?

At its core, mindfulness involves focusing all your attention on the present moment. Regardless of what happened earlier or what might happen later, the present moment is where you are right now. We don't spend our lives in the past or the future; we spend our lives in the present.

Many of us live our lives in our minds, allowing thoughts of past events and thoughts of future events to overshadow the joy of experiencing the present moment. This is especially unhelpful when our thoughts make us feel uneasy, irritated, miserable and despondent. It's such a shame because we're missing out on the beauty of what's happening now; we're missing out on large chunks of our lives.

Many of our present moments are spoilt by our speculating and over-analytical minds: judging, complaining, approving, disapproving and, worst of all, worrying. The majority of our thinking is of little use. It goes round in circles and is often negative. If you stop thinking and calm your mind, even for a few seconds or minutes, you will begin to see the world more clearly.

Notice your thoughts

We all have a natural inclination to overthink. As I mention in Chapter 34, one useful thing we can do is to observe our thoughts as they unintentionally pop into our heads. Try not to evaluate them and try not to let them take over. Imagine they belong to another person and just observe them. Be on the lookout for repetitive thought patterns.

Through observation, your thoughts eventually lose their intensity and control over you because the mind slowly weakens its bond with them. The simple act of observing your thoughts can help you separate from them: you're no longer living in your thoughts but merely observing them.

Let go of your story

We all have our own story that explains where we came from, who we are now and what we would like to do in the future. This story helps us describe who we are to the outside world, but it's incredibly constraining because it's also a device that we use to lie to ourselves. The ego keeps us thinking and talking about this story because the ego wants nothing more than to be admired. If, however, we let go of our story, we're free to be our authentic self. We wouldn't care about looking stupid or being self-conscious because we wouldn't feel the need to impress anyone or live in our story any longer.

Living in the present moment forces you to forget your story and ask yourself, 'What could I focus on right now to feel connected to this moment and thankful for it?' The more often you consider this question, the easier it becomes to live in this moment and the next. Ask this question as often as possible; make it a habit.

We use our life story to attach labels to ourselves. We also attach labels to other people, even when we know little about them. We describe ourselves and others as wealthy or poor, intelligent or stupid, happy or depressed, kind or unkind, a success or a failure. These labels are just labels. They don't describe or define who we are, and we shouldn't let them have an impact on our lives. For example, you might describe yourself as an ambitious entrepreneur who needs to spend 80 hours a week at work. But does this label prevent you from spending time on things that bring joy into your life? Would you prefer to be doing other things such as spending time with your family and friends or enjoying other simple pleasures.

Mindful meditation

By far the most common and effective mindfulness practice is meditation. MRI scans of people who'd taken a mindfulness meditation course for eight weeks showed that their brain's amygdala had shrunk, whereas their brain's prefrontal cortex had become thicker. This is generally good news because the amygdala is responsible for fear, emotion and stress, whereas the prefrontal cortex is responsible for higher order brain functions such as awareness, impulse control, creativity, comprehension and problem solving.

Try This: There are no hard and fast rules for meditating, but to get started I would recommend the following:

- Find a comfortable and relaxed sitting position.

- Take a few slow, deep breaths.
- Slowly allow your breathing to return to its natural rhythm and intensity.
- Continue to focus your entire attention on your breathing, whether it is the rise and fall of your chest or the sensation of air coming in and out of your mouth and nose. If you notice your attention has drifted, slowly bring it back to your breath.

Do this for 10 minutes, or however much time feels right for you.

For most of us, 100 per cent thought free meditation is very difficult, if not impossible, especially in the first few sessions. It's highly unusual for a novice to concentrate solely on the breath for more than 10 seconds at a time, so don't be disheartened; this is quite normal. When thoughts come into your mind, don't try to control them or block them. Instead, simply allow them to come and go. Then return your focus back to your breathing.

Thoughts will relentlessly appear from nowhere, but every time you notice and observe these thoughts, you're on the right track. With time and persistence, the frequency and intensity of your thoughts will diminish. Don't worry if you think you're not making progress – excellence is not the purpose. Simply enjoy the peace. Enjoy the serenity.

While meditating, you might find it useful to think or quietly say to yourself, 'May I be happy, may I be calm, may I have tranquillity'. Say this a few times and then change it a little, 'May my loved ones be happy, may they be calm, may they have tranquillity'. By incorporating other people, you're opening your heart and extending your love to others: 'May XYZ be happy, may they be calm, may they have tranquillity', 'May my adversaries be happy, may they be calm, may they have tranquillity'.

Try This: A body survey is another effective way to meditate. The purpose of the body survey is to tune into your body and to make a mental connection with your physical self. Here's how it works:

- Find a comfortable position.
- Spend two minutes just breathing. As before, focus only on your breathing.
- Bring awareness to each part of your body, one area at a time. Begin by observing any sensations you have in your feet and toes, then move to your calves, knees, thighs, groin, torso, shoulders, arms, hands and fingers, neck and head.
- Finish off by spending two minutes just breathing naturally.

The overall goal of any meditation is to experience a period without thoughts. To begin with, these periods will be just a second or two, but with time they'll expand to five seconds, and then 10 seconds, and so on. When these short periods occur, you'll feel tranquillity and harmony inside, and with repetition this sense of tranquillity and harmony will intensify. To get the most out of your meditation, it is therefore important to find a regular time for it. Begin with 10 minutes a day and see where that takes you.

Mindfulness as you go about your day

Another aim of mindfulness is to be wholly engaged with and immersed in whatever you're doing at any given moment, whether it is walking, driving, cleaning, cooking or eating. If you strip out everything that isn't solely the action in which you're engaged, you're now meditating.

For example, when walking, few of us pay much attention to our body's movement or the world around us. Walking is usually just a means for us to get from one place to another while we think about something else. Instead of being preoccupied with your mind, however, try paying attention to the variety of visuals, sounds and smells around you, the sensations that you've long stopped noticing.

Living mindfully simply involves giving your full attention to your breath, to your movement, to your environs, to other people, to your activities, to the wonders of nature, engineering and architecture; not to influence them or be troubled by them, but simply to notice and experience them. Watch young children playing. Notice how they live in the present, observing, interacting and having fun with the world. As adults we can learn a great deal from children simply by being alert, aware and interested in what's going on around us.

One thing at a time

How often do you multitask? You might think it saves valuable time, but frantic lifestyles and multitasking make our minds overactive and stressed. For example, we think we use our devices to save time, but far too often they make us more anxious as message after message comes through while we're doing something else. Chronic multitaskers find it impossible to relax and enjoy the present moment because their attention is scattered here, there and everywhere. All of the so-called productivity benefits of multitasking are negated by an extra layer of frenetic anxiety which adds to our daily burden of minor stressors.

Begin making a new habit of doing just one thing at a time and be fully committed to it (even something seemingly monotonous like mowing the lawn or cleaning the kitchen). Savour the experience. Rather than treat it as a means to an end, treat it as an 'end' in its own right. Treat it as a type of meditation and watch your thoughts, especially when your thoughts make you feel stressed. Gently bring your mind back to the present moment and refocus on whatever it is that you're doing.

Happy right here, right now

Do you often wish you were somewhere else? On a beach? In a different job? Living with someone else? The truth is, happiness has to come from within you, not outside of you, so if you're unhappy now, the chances are that you'll be unhappy whatever you do or wherever you go. By concentrating more on being content with where you are, you have a great chance of finding happiness here and now.

We often spend weeks, months, sometimes years working toward a big goal. We think, 'when I achieve this goal, I will finally feel happy'. When we reduce our lives to a compulsive need to reach, to achieve, to succeed, we cease to see, hear, taste, smell and savour the magnificence of what's happening right now. Consider the following questions:

- Are your daily activities just a means to an end? Or do you enjoy them?
- Is happiness waiting for you in the future? Or are you happy right now?
- Are you obsessed with completing, accomplishing, winning, owning or pursuing some new indulgence that will make you more content? Or are you happy right now?
- Are you currently in pursuit of more possessions, money, success, power or recognition so you can feel more complete? Or are you happy right now?
- Is your imaginary 'happy' future an escape from your 'unhappy' present?

Many people keep rescheduling their happiness. They persuade themselves that they'll be happier next month or next year. What a waste of our short time here on this planet. If this is you, don't waste another minute – find a way to be happy right now!

How much of a problem are your problems?

Problems and difficulties are an inevitable part of life, so try to look at them as 'circumstances' that may or may not need some attention. These circumstances can be dealt with now or later, or simply noted and left alone as part of what is. Don't carry around a long list in your head of all the things you have to do. For each item, either do it now or put a note in your diary to do it later. Always consider the option of doing nothing.

Mindful arguing

Do you ever feel a strong need to win an argument? Do you get upset when someone makes a harmless joke about you? This is your ego at work. When our ego is threatened, we defend or attack or both. If this is you, learn to notice your feelings and observe how your ego makes you react. Simply observing your ego's defensive reaction will help you question it and then distance yourself from it. Detaching from your ego in this way will make you less likely to engage in one upmanship, which is ultimately damaging to your relationships. The moment the ego stops, it creates space for love, joy and harmony.

Sometimes it may be appropriate to talk about an aspect of someone's conduct but do it without having to be right or them having to be wrong – it's not a competition. Our ego is both resilient and calculating, however, so we need to be very alert and honest with ourselves to catch it in the heat of battle. Make a conscious effort to listen to the other person attentively without your ego interfering or attempting to take over. When your ego lays down its weapons, genuine, honest and open dialogue can begin.

Live in the present, not the past or the future

Do past events fill your mind? Do these thoughts involve blame, shame, injustice, bitterness, rage or remorse? Do you speculate and worry about future events? Virtually everyone fills their mind with the past and future virtually all of the time, so much so that there is no room left for the now. Whenever you notice that this is happening, refocus your attention on the present moment and enjoy it.

Accept your feelings

When some people have an unpleasant feeling, such as sadness, fear or shame, their first reaction is to reject that feeling. They don't want to have this feeling, so they try to push it away, or they use drugs or alcohol to help them feel better. The problem is, when we reject our emotions and feelings in this way, we are probably making things worse for ourselves. Our feelings and emotions exist because they give us valuable and helpful information about the world; information that we shouldn't ignore.

If you feel fear or rage, don't dismiss it or resist it because you want it to go away. Feel it and observe it without categorising it. We all have unwanted emotions, but they are always temporary and they will always pass. Be present in your feelings and emotions and you'll see how non-resistance transforms misery into acceptance and then into peace.

Remember: If you live in complete acknowledgement and acceptance of what is, you'll be better equipped to analyse any difficult situation calmly. When adversity strikes, you will typically have three options:

- Accept the situation.
- Remove yourself from the situation.
- Work out what you can do to improve the situation.

It often appears as though an external situation is creating our suffering, but this isn't so – our internal resistance is the cause of our suffering. With this wisdom, we can live in a state of grace, kindness and peace. We can liberate ourselves from the continuous struggle.

Remember that yesterday is history and tomorrow is a mystery. But today is a gift, so enjoy it before it's gone.

46

SOCIAL SKILLS

Build your ability to get on with people.

We've evolved to pursue the companionship of others because in ancient times belonging to a group of other humans was central to our survival. Modern humans still need to belong; to be accepted by a group – a group where they are valued. For those who fail to satisfy this fundamental need for connection and approval, life can be tough because above all else we fear rejection and crave acceptance. Humans are social animals, and we grow and thrive when we have many high-quality connections with our family, friends and acquaintances.

While some people have a natural ability to build rapport with a variety of people, others find it a struggle. It would be an oversimplification to attribute this variance to whether someone is an extrovert or introvert, or whether someone is confident or shy. Being a confident extrovert will, admittedly, help you find new friends, but it won't necessarily help you build genuine and lasting bonds. For that you need good social skills.

Talking to others

If you would like to start up a conversation with someone, don't worry too much about how you will be received because most people will welcome you making the effort to reach out to them. Just smile and introduce yourself or casually strike up a conversation about something that's happening around you. It normally takes just one comment to get started and after that the conversation will take on a life of its own.

Once you're chatting, show a genuine interest in the person: their family, their origins, their occupation, their interests, etc. People tend to gravitate toward people who share common interests, so seek these out by asking plenty of questions. People love talking about themselves and you're paying them a huge compliment by simply listening to what they have to say. Try to learn their name and use it in conversation as this further enhances your image as a sincere, kind and friendly person. Try to be interested, not interesting, and search out commonalities between your outlook and theirs, while displaying attentiveness through your facial expressions and body language.

Begin to view your interactions with others as a journey of discovery, and embrace this journey with an open mind, using it as an opportunity to learn something new and make new connections. When people genuinely connect, they see the world through each other's eyes and use each other's ideas and opinions as a foundation to create something truly meaningful.

Advanced Empathetic listening

Empathetic listening means giving the other person your undivided attention. It means asking questions and paraphrasing their words, so you fully understand everything they're saying. It means immersing yourself in the activities and opinions of others without being disapproving.

Empathetic listening will help you truly 'get' someone and establish a closer bond. It shows that you care and helps them to feel valued and understood. It encourages trust. Parents, for example, often make the mistake of listening disapprovingly rather than listening empathetically. They often react critically or try to solve their child's problems themselves, a strategy which fails to give the child a feeling that they're being heard on an emotional level. Sometimes children might need guidance, but sometimes they just need an empathetic ear. Adults are no different.

Mirror people

Highly empathetic individuals frequently mirror the people around them. They copy the body language, facial expressions and sometimes the emotions of their conversation partners. Mirroring is hardwired into our minds: brain cells called mirror neurons are thought to support observational learning and promote imitation of those around us. They allow us to reciprocate other people's actions and the feelings behind those actions. When you see someone smile, for example, your mirror neurons for smiling are activated and you smile back. Mirror neurons subconsciously encourage us to placate people and they are a vital ingredient in the glue that binds us all together.

Pitfalls to avoid

When it comes to forming connections, there are a few obstacles we need to avoid:

- **The need to be cooler than others:** It's okay to be 'uncool'. Just as you welcome other people being unguarded and candid with you, your honesty and readiness to expose your true self will be welcomed by others. Letting yourself be vulnerable in this way shows humility. The occasions when we truly bond with other people are those in which we reveal ourselves honestly; not being cool, just being ourselves. (See Chapter 40 on peer pressure.)
- **The need to exaggerate:** You may overstate routine events as 'awesome' or average people as 'legendary' in order to get an approving response or to amaze people. Unfortunately, this can be counterproductive as it diminishes the full impact of

the word, making it far less impressive when something really is 'awesome'.

- **The need to be right:** Ask yourself, 'Do I have to be right all the time or can I handle situations more sensitively?' Constantly fighting our corner can be draining and it usually distances us from people. Unless it's absolutely necessary, resist the temptation to correct people and give them the freedom to express themselves in their own words – even if there are a few minor errors in their train of thought. Try to understand them on a deeper level, rather than getting caught up in minutiae.

- **The need to please others:** Whilst it's important to remain empathetic, your message can suffer if you're overly concerned with people-pleasing and agreeing with everything you hear no matter what. You may well be seen as inauthentic and find that people don't take you seriously.

Compliments, praise and gratitude

How frequently do you tell someone how much you respect or value them? How frequently do other people compliment or praise you? The answer to both questions is probably not often enough. Most people love to be appreciated and valued, so a genuine compliment is a real gift that costs nothing to give. People are generally pleasantly surprised and grateful when you use compliments or praise in a positive and proactive way, so don't be shy – make a habit of saying something nice to at least one person every day.

Another very effective way to create bonds is to show gratitude, so whenever the occasion arises, take the time to thank someone for their help. This will make them feel respected and appreciated. (See Chapter 52 for more on Gratitude.)

Eye contact and smiling

From time to time we come across people who move around with their head bowed, avoiding eye contact and generally looking at odds with the world. It's highly unlikely that these people are covertly serene and happy, so what can we learn from them?

Firstly, eye contact is very important to most people, so it won't work in your favour if you avoid it. Secondly, smiles are contagious, so spread them around generously – but be careful not to fake it. Authentic smiles make our cheeks rise, forming wrinkles – sometimes called laughter lines – around our eyes. A real smile lights up the whole face.

Remember: Social situations come in all shapes and sizes and there isn't a right or wrong way to deal with any of them. However, if you try out some of the advice in this chapter, most social settings will become easier to handle. Proactively go after the outcomes you desire, and through trial and error you'll soon learn to navigate the multifaceted subtleties of social interaction more naturally.

47

ROMANTIC RELATIONSHIPS

Nurture your relationship with your partner.

The more effort we put into cultivating close, meaningful relationships, the happier we tend to be. This applies to friendships and relationships with family members, but especially to romantic relationships.

Statistically speaking, secure and rewarding romantic relationships have a big influence on our happiness. The National Opinion Research Center in Chicago surveyed 35,000 Americans over a 30-year period. 40 per cent of married people said they were 'very happy' while only 24 per cent of unmarried, separated and widowed people said this. The major caveat here is that people who are already happy are more likely to get married and stay married, but there is still a comfortable consensus in social sciences that marriage or similar long-term relationships have a positive and enduring effect on happiness. This correlation makes sense because when you're loved for exactly who you are, you're free to express your true self.

Please note that these are just statistics and I'm not suggesting that all single people should rush out into the world and get married. If you're single you could be one of those 24 per cent of people who are 'very happy' without a partner. The main reason for presenting these statistics is to illustrate that if you are in a relationship, there's a good chance that it's worth staying in it, and it's therefore worth making the effort to make it as harmonious and fulfilling as possible.

Pleasure and meaning

To be successful, romantic relationships need to have both pleasure and meaning in equal measure. Pleasure-seeking relationships relying on only sex rapidly lose their meaning, while relationships heavily centred on common values but devoid of fun and desire might lose their spark.

When we share our life with someone, we invite them to share their life with us. Building a shared life together involves both partners supporting each other and freely communicating their opinions, emotions and experiences with each other. Sharing the good times is easy and fun, but when a partner supports you during the bad times, that's when you know you have found that rare but good relationship. The need to be loved, appreciated and valued is deeply rooted in human nature.

Compatibility, intimacy and stability

What is romantic love to you and your partner? Experts define the first phase of a loving relationship as the 'in love' phase. This is the infatuated and involuntary phase of love, whereby everything else in our lives pales into insignificance. The average duration of the 'in love' phase is around two years, so why and how do most couples maintain loving relationships that last much longer?

All solid loving relationships have three fundamental characteristics:

- **Compatibility.** This is the bedrock upon which your relationship is built. Do you have similar values? Do you have shared goals and desires, and on a practical level, do you have shared activities? We all change and therefore our compatibility changes with age, but so long as our core values and life expectations don't change dramatically over time then our compatibility will remain a key asset to the relationship.

- **Intimacy.** There are four different kinds of intimacy:

  o *Emotional* intimacy – how easily do you express emotions to each other. Do you feel safe sharing your feelings, even uncomfortable ones?

o *Intellectual* intimacy – how well do you understand and empathise with the way your partner thinks and forms opinions. Do you feel comfortable sharing opinions and ideas, even when you disagree?

o *Physical* intimacy – how well do you bond through physical contact or sex?

o *Experiential* intimacy – how well do you bond during leisure activities? Shared experiences lead to inside jokes and private memories that can intensify a connection.

- **Stability.** This depends on how harmoniously you communicate each and every day. This is vital because your sense of connection will rapidly diminish if exposed to regular arguments and irritations.

Positive interactions to focus on

Communication

Keeping love in a relationship that's moved past the initial stage depends heavily on successful communication. This means outlining our preferences for the relationship and finding the best way to communicate these preferences with our partner.

It's rare for a person's communication style to always correspond exactly with that of their partner, and disagreements of varying magnitude will undoubtedly arise, even between long-term partners. Harmony is crucial to a stable relationship and according to relationship researcher John Gottman, good interactions need to outnumber bad interactions by at least five to one. We therefore need to keep a watchful eye on the frequency and intensity of those bad interactions, so try to shift your thinking toward what's good in your relationship, rather than what's bad.

Praise and gratitude

Look out for appropriate situations to offer compliments and other kind words of reinforcement – they're sure to be well received. If the praise is mixed with gratitude, such as a 'thank you' for a wonderful meal, then you and your partner's mutual appreciation will be given a massive boost. The benefits are especially strong when a partner appreciates a positive character attribute, like being intelligent, caring or kind-hearted. This is really helpful when it comes to minimising the importance of a partner's bad habits – 'accentuate the positive, eliminate the negative' – as the song goes!

Quality time

Spending quality time together is vital, but what exactly do we mean by this? Firstly, we don't mean just being in the same room as each other – that doesn't count. You need to centre your attention toward your partner and ignore everything else, even when multiple distractions are at play. Giving your full attention to your partner makes them feel valued and cherished. Quality time means meaningful conversations and shared experiences, anything from walking and chatting to shared hobbies, or simply making dinner together.

A little fun and adventure will also add a bit of zest to most relationships. Explore together, travel together, go to a cookery class together, act a bit silly together. Couples who regularly play and laugh together form stronger bonds, and the more shared experiences they have, the more they can enjoy reminiscing together.

Gifts

For many people receiving gifts is highly pleasurable, and when a gift is given from one partner to another, it is an expression of affection irrespective of monetary value. Over the years you should become familiar with what type of gift your partner likes, but if you're at a loss for fresh ideas, ask family and friends or do a little internet searching. The significance of any gift is embedded in the entire process: the thought, the idea, the purchase, the wrapping and finally the handing over to your partner. You don't have to wait for Christmas or birthdays and the gift doesn't have to cost the earth. If you see something appropriate, just buy it and give it.

Little acts of kindness

Does your partner often wish you would clean up after meals, empty the bins or do other household chores? It's a kind gesture to do a helpful thing for your partner, so if a job needs to be done why not just do it, even if it's not necessarily your job or your turn. Do little acts of kindness regularly; things you know your partner will appreciate you doing. And avoid keeping a mental tally of who is contributing the most – it shouldn't be about keeping score to establish superiority. When things go wrong you might need to carry out much bigger acts of kindness. Standing by your partner during hard times is vital, so commit to being front and centre when the going gets tough.

Physical affection

Physical affection is an important part of any healthy relationship. Kissing, cuddling and sex are obviously great ways to communicate affection, but small things like putting your arm around your partner or a simple touch will often be welcomed and can be done every day. Also, if you do some of these things around other people, it will feel a little more special to your partner. Maybe not the sex though!

Negative interactions – handle with care!

Accept your differences

No two people are the same. You and your partner will behave differently, express emotions differently, and have different preferences with respect to things like food, drink, leisure activities and the friends that you keep. This is perfectly normal so it's important to understand these dissimilarities rather than trying to force your partner to change. Learning about your partner's preferences can also make your relationship more interesting. Maybe you were nervous of spicy food until your partner encouraged you to try out Indian food. When you have clear differences in taste or opinion, try to remain curious and find out more before opposing or judging.

Stop and think before disagreeing

Timing is critical, so before you begin a potentially volatile exchange of views, stop and consider the best time and place to have your disagreement. Also consider your strategy. Are you willing to stay calm and listen attentively with an open mind? Are you happy to consider making any changes or compromises? For more on dealing with conflict, see Chapter 42.

Avoid personal attacks

Poor communication often happens when our language and tone of voice builds walls instead of bridges. Try not to make generalised personal accusations if your partner makes a mistake. For example, calling your partner 'forgetful' when they forget something is making a personal attack and they'll probably be defensive in response. Other high-minded judgements, insults and generalisations are also unhelpful.

How do you feel and why?

When you're frustrated or irritated, instead of lashing out, try to identify what's causing these feelings for you – what do you want to be different and why? For example, you might want to see a clean kitchen every time you walk into it because you like to begin preparing food without having to clean the kitchen first. So how can you encourage your partner to help keep the kitchen clean without accusing, blaming or hurting their feelings. In this situation, you could try a candid but compassionate request: 'David, when I see a messy kitchen, I feel discouraged from cooking us a lovely meal because I have to tidy and clean the kitchen before I can start. Would you be willing to help me keep the kitchen clean and tidy?'

Establish rules and preferences

We get upset with people when they challenge our rules and preferences. We cannot, however, expect our preferences to be the same as everyone else, so we need to tell people what's important to us. If your partner keeps leaving the lights switched on throughout the house, tell them how this makes you feel and offer a feasible solution: 'Leaving the lights on upsets me because it wastes money and it isn't particularly good for the planet. Can you try to remember to switch them off when you leave an empty room. It would mean a lot to me, and it could save us quite a lot of money over a whole year?'

Of course, this process isn't one-way, so you should also make an effort to learn your partner's rules and do whatever you can to accommodate them.

Observe without generalising

Observing without generalising will reduce defensiveness, so try to avoid 'You always' or 'You never' statements. For example, a phrase like 'You always get home late' is a generalisation, whereas 'Last Tuesday and Thursday you arrived home after 9 p.m.' is an observation. Similarly, 'You never unload the dishwasher' is a generalisation, but a more accurate observation would be 'I've unloaded the dishwasher for the last five times in a row'. Both observations here are specific and free of criticism, so your partner has no need to get defensive. Also, try not to use negative labels such as 'lazy' or 'selfish'. Instead, take the time to find the words to describe your observations both clearly and respectfully.

Paraphrase and question

If your partner raises a point of contention, it's important to make sure that you fully understand it. The best way to do this is to paraphrase your understanding of what they've said back to them: 'You think that I don't do enough to help with the kids when I get home from work?' This shows that you're listening and you're trying to understand the problem. It also gives your partner an opportunity to correct any misunderstanding or add more detail: 'Yes, I'm usually tired by the time you get home and the kids know how to push all my buttons at mealtimes.' This is very positive communication because your partner clearly has a problem with the kids and not with you. You've reduced defensiveness and maximised the likelihood of a mutually satisfactory solution. You could then say, 'What can I do to help?'

By paraphrasing and questioning in this way, you help both you and your partner fully understand what the problem is and hopefully you can resolve it together. While we all like to hear those three wonderful words 'I love you', I would argue that the three words 'Tell me more' are just as powerful.

Silence, time outs and ultimatums

Don't just cease to communicate by stopping listening and staying silent. It's childish, rude and goes against the spirit of mature, loving communication. By listening and being receptive, you'll make your partner feel like you acknowledge and value their feelings. This may or may not help but staying silent will almost certainly make things worse.

If your partner's grievances are about to overwhelm you and you feel you're going to get into a row, you might be better served by taking a time out. Separate yourself physically from the situation and find a place where you can be alone. This will give you time to calm down and reflect. You can then continue the conversation later with a cool head.

Don't let a little dispute injure a great relationship and never ever threaten the future of the relationship with ultimatums.

Remember: Romance endures when you value your partner during the monotony of daily life, so don't take everyday conversations for granted. Make your relationship one of your highest priorities and in the amended words of a famous JF Kennedy quote, 'ask not what your relationship can do for you, but what you can do for your relationship'.

48

AGEING

Are you concerned about getting old?

Well, you shouldn't be! In today's youth-obsessed culture, more and more people associate ageing with losing beauty and even losing love and respect. It's important that you don't let yourself succumb to these superficial ageing concerns, as there are so many positives that come with age.

Positive changes in our later years

In some areas of life, we actually improve as we age:

- **Positive brain developments:** Due to plaque build-up in the brain and a reduction in neurochemicals and dopamine, our mental capabilities do slow as we age. At the same time, however, we experience new, positive changes in the brain. For example, a biochemical transformation occurs that makes it easier for us to acknowledge and accept death. Also, the amygdala loses much of its intensity, and as a result we experience less fear and become more emotionally balanced and secure.

- **Better practical intelligence and perceptual completion:** In studies, people over the age of 50 score the highest in practical intelligence and perceptual completion. Practical intelligence is garnered from a lifetime of experience – the older you are, the better you are at coming up with solutions to everyday problems. Perceptual completion is related to filling in the blind spots that life continually throws at us. Imagine that you're driving along and you pass a sign at the side of the road, but because of your road position and speed, you only see the words 'Farm Shpp'. Your brain automatically turns 'Shpp' into 'Shop' because of the setting and context of the situation. Our minds are regularly making these leaps, and the minds of older people tend to do better at filling in these details.

Our vocabulary and crystallised intelligence (accumulated knowledge) both peak in our 60s and 70s and older brains perform better when making decisions based on pattern recognition or when encountering complicated circumstances. Older brains are also better at remembering prior circumstances and the connections their brains made at the time. This makes older people better at stepping back to observe the big picture when it comes to difficult decisions – so if you have a question that requires detachment, objectivity and wisdom, ask an older adult for guidance.

More forgetful?

How often do you hear old age linked with forgetfulness? These assumptions are misleading because memory function is far more multifaceted than most people think. There is a small drop in memory performance for 8.5 per cent of those aged 65 to 70, but people of all ages experience short-term memory lapses. When we're young, we tend to pay little attention to it, but when older people experience short-term memory loss, they have been primed to believe it's due to cognitive deterioration, maybe referring to it as a 'senior moment'. Also, older people can reduce memory decline by keeping physically and mentally active.

Perspective on time

When we're in our twenties, we're mostly living in the present and future, with much of our life ahead of us. In our thirties, forties and fifties, we're living through the busiest period of our life, and we mostly live in the present, with a little drifting into the past and future from time to time.

As we age further, we begin to live more in the present and past, often recollecting triumphs and troubles from years gone by. The majority of our life is behind us and our most significant highlights, such as leaving school, major career milestones, getting married and having a family are no longer future events but have been converted into past remembrances. The past gets longer; the future gets shorter. With less time and fewer key milestones to look forward to we feel that time goes faster, and we might fret about the small amount of time we have remaining to fulfil our dreams.

Older people also experience role losses; their role as a parent diminishes, they withdraw from their role in the workplace and certain leisure activities become untenable. At this stage their previously dynamic impact on society is tapering down. The brain's inner chronometer ticks away at a slower cadence such that the brain counts less time than when we were younger, which is why time appears to pass quicker with age.

So what can we do about this? The simple answer is to make a wide variety of new memories, and lots of them. The brain loves new things, so immerse yourself in a multiplicity of new information, new experiences and new activities every day. You could enrol in a new course or learn a new skill. You could visit some new places and attend various events, all the time exposing yourself to a multitude of like-minded new people.

Remember: Stop letting people tell you you're supposed to slow down as you get older. Stay passionate and engaged and exercise as much as your body allows. Also, pass your skills and knowledge back into the world: volunteer, join a club or mentor a younger person. Your experience could be incredibly useful to many different people. It's never too late to be who you want to be and do the things you want to do.

49

MONEY

How do you feel about money?

Does having more money actually make you happier? If the answer is yes, do you know why that is? A study by researchers at Cardiff University and the University of Warwick found that money can make people happier if it improves their social rank. The researchers found that simply being highly paid wasn't enough – to be happy, people must perceive themselves as being more highly paid than their friends and work colleagues. In cultures that encourage too much competition, however, people often go all out to outdo each other. This win or lose mentality will also have a knock-on effect on the overall happiness of these societies, with many disadvantaged individuals being left behind.

In general, people living in richer countries are happier than those living in very poor countries, because poverty and political instability are massively unfavourable to leading a happy and comfortable life. But only up to a point. The positive effects of having more money cease to exist once families achieve enough financial security to cover their basic needs. A 2010 Princeton University study established that emotional well-being does rise with income, but there is no further progress beyond an annual income of around $75,000 per annum for an average US household. The study concludes that high income buys life satisfaction, but not happiness.

While having plenty of money doesn't necessarily make you happier, what you do with it might make all the difference – with big emphasis on the word 'do'. A 2014 study by Thomas Gilovich et al (Cornell University) indicates that 'experiential' purchases (buying experiences) provide greater satisfaction and happiness because:

- Experiential purchases enhance social relationships more readily and effectively than purchasing material goods, because they enrich social bonding through sharing common activities. We go on holiday with friends and family, and go to restaurants, concerts and sporting events with like-minded people.

- Experiential purchases form a bigger part of a person's identity. People enjoy talking about experiences more than material goods. If you were asked to write your memoirs, you'd probably write much more about your life experiences than the things you've purchased.

- Experiential purchases are evaluated more on their own terms and evoke fewer social comparisons and one-upmanship than material purchases.

Another way to spend money to bring you happiness is to spend money on other people. A 2020 study, by Elizabeth Dunn et al, found that spending money on others – prosocial spending – can bring more happiness than spending money on yourself. This can be in the form of a gift to a friend or a charitable donation. Prosocial spending enhances happiness on multiple levels:

- Spending money on others enhances feelings of social connection, which is an important catalyst in turning good deeds into good feelings.

- Spending money on others provides an opportunity to make a meaningful impact, satisfying our need to feel capable and competent. This is especially so when we are able to directly see the difference our generosity makes for the person or cause we are helping.

- Because autonomy is critical for personal well-being, people derive more joy from spending money on others when they are free to choose whether to help or not.

The same study also found that happiness can be improved by buying time. For example, paying others to do jobs that we don't want to do ourselves or buying labour-saving devices such as washing machines, robot vacuum cleaners and robot lawn mowers.

Psychology of investing

So far in this chapter, I've focused solely on acquiring and spending money, but what about investing money for the future? Most of us would be well served to seek plenty of independent advice on this matter because when it comes to investing, we're not always as rational as we think we are – the average investor consistently fails to exceed or even match the broader market indices. Why does this happen? Behavioural investing research throws up some interesting explanations.

Beware overconfidence

Humans notoriously overate their capabilities in many facets of life, and this overconfidence can persuade financial investors to make big mistakes. Our investment brains are often not quite the stable, proficient and analytical instruments we think they are. Thinking positively can be beneficial, but overconfidence is counterproductive and can end in disastrous consequences.

We often think the future is predictable because all outcomes make sense with hindsight, and if we think we know why things happened in the past, we believe we have the wherewithal to foresee the future. Also, an early run of winners makes us believe we have control over somewhat random outcomes, which in turn leads us to believe that our own strategies are better than those of others.

Ask questions

Be mindful that your analysis of investment risk isn't always consistent or robust. It will vary according to:

- Your memory of previous investments
- Whether you're investing in a group or alone
- How manageable the risk 'feels' to you
- How it's presented and explained
- What mood you're in at the time

For example, a financial advisor can persuade you to accept or avoid risk just by changing how they explain it. A retirement plan might have an 80 per cent chance of meeting your retirement objectives. The same plan has a 20 per cent chance of failing to meet your retirement objectives. One of these descriptions sounds positive and the other sounds negative, but they're in fact describing the same retirement plan.

For this reason always critique any data given to you, and analyse that data from different angles, generally being more pessimistic than optimistic. Take your time, ask lots of questions and seek a second opinion from someone prepared to challenge your assumptions. The higher the profit that an investment claims to target, the more questions you should ask.

Also, be wary of multiple layers of fees and be sure to calculate their impact on investment returns.

Let the data speak

The most successful investors seek out many pieces of information. They are detailed and thorough, considering issues from several standpoints and prudently evaluating advantages and disadvantages. They seek reliable evidence, do background checks and rarely act on intuition alone. They learn from their successes and failures and adjust their strategy accordingly.

Bargain-hunting

The investing environment is highly irregular and situations rarely repeat themselves precisely, so your investment philosophy needs to be adaptable – it's actually during the worst of times that we learn the most. During the good times, investors are less afraid of risk and they buy assets at high prices. Some investors perpetually buy at the top and then sell at the bottom in that moment of maximum fear. This is often a mistake because a share price or asset that's just fallen through the roof is much cheaper and therefore of more interest than it was before it fell.

The advantage of buying something for less than it's worth is obvious, and for a long-term value investor a low entry price is an excellent starting point as it lowers risk at the outset. The best under-priced assets are found in special situations or involve doing things other investors can't or won't do, or when dealing with a distressed or forced seller. The goal here isn't to find good assets, but good under-priced assets. Bargains providing value at unreasonably low prices are the Holy Grail for investors.

Remember: The most successful investors focus on longterm investments that they understand. And they do not put all their eggs into one basket – diversification is crucial. Before investing your hard-earned money, set your budget, do plenty of research, get plenty of advice and don't rush it.

50

TRUST AND FORGIVENESS

Learn to trust and forgive.

Has anyone ever done you a big favour, but you suspected that they had an ulterior motive? Have you been let down by an individual so badly that it affects the way you trust everyone else? Humans are naturally suspicious because evolution has taught us that mistrusting people helps keep us alive. In the modern era life and death is less of an issue but we still use mistrust to protect ourselves from a multitude of things such as physical harm, fraud, or even heartbreak.

If you lost a wallet full of credit cards and money in the street, do you think a passer-by would return it to you including all the cash and cards? In one experiment, random people in Toronto were asked this question and only 25 per cent said yes. Researchers then dropped identical wallets containing money, bank cards and an emergency telephone number around various parts of the city and a massive 80 per cent were returned to the owner with the full amount of cash intact! This implies that our trust in other people should be higher than it is.

Learning through trust

People who trust the media are more knowledgeable about politics and current affairs. People who trust science are more scientifically literate and make better decisions regarding their health, nutrition and many other things. The more we trust, the more we learn about which individuals and organisations we can trust in the future.

If you find it difficult to trust people, begin by trusting them in small ways and build from there. There will always be bumps in the road, but if you fail to trust anyone and stay in your bubble, you'll miss out on so many mutually beneficial relationships and opportunities.

Are you trustworthy?

Try This: Let's not forget that trust works both ways, so take a minute to reflect on your own trustworthiness:

- Are you reliable? Do you always do what you say you're going to do, or do you regularly turn up late, cancel appointments or miss deadlines?
- Do you take responsibility for your mistakes, or do you blame others or blame circumstances?

- Do you respect other people's boundaries? Do you know when to back off, or do you invite yourself into situations where you might not be that welcome? Are you just plain nosey?

- Do you keep other people's confidential information to yourself? You'll certainly lose the trust of others if you gain a reputation for spreading gossip.

- Do you make decisions with honesty and integrity? Do you treat other people with honesty and integrity?

- Are you tolerant and supportive of others, or do you have plenty of negative things to say about them?

- Are you generous? This doesn't have to mean financial generosity; it could be generosity with possessions, favours, advice or time.

Think about your answers to these questions and then honestly evaluate how much trust you deserve to get from others.

The power of forgiveness

Anger, hatred and bitterness are damaging emotions that do not serve us well. When you direct these emotions toward other people, you erect a barricade around yourself and become imprisoned by your own hurt, self-righteousness or self-pity. Your relationships will suffer and ultimately you will suffer as a result. The only way to rise above this negative energy is to forgive.

If someone lets you down, as they inevitably will, begin with a compassionate attitude and try to appreciate their side of the story – what is driving their behaviour? Maybe this behaviour has something to do with their anxieties and insecurities? The more we understand other people and their motives, the easier it is to forgive them.

Psychologists generally define forgiveness as a conscious and deliberate choice to release feelings of resentment or retaliation toward a person or group who has harmed us in some way, irrespective of whether they deserve our forgiveness. Forgiveness means casting away our accusations; it means less confrontation and more going with the flow.

Practising forgiveness can also have potent health benefits. Observational analyses and some randomised trials suggest that forgiveness is associated with lower levels of depression, anxiety and hostility; reduced substance abuse; higher self-worth; and increased happiness.

Forgiveness toward another person happens when you realise that your anger serves no purpose, except to bolster your ego, which can't function without strife and conflict. If someone says something that's disrespectful or designed to hurt, try to let it pass over your head without opposition or defiance. If it's necessary, tell the person that their behaviour is offensive, but don't let it affect your inner calm. Stay cool.

When you forgive, you can still distance yourself from that person if you choose to. Forgiveness means no longer needing punishment, retribution or reparation; it means no longer reliving the past, but moving on, unburdened.

Forgiveness also applies to your own wrongdoings. If you forgive yourself, it'll also make it easier for you to forgive others.

A meditation for forgiveness

Try This: If you struggle with forgiveness, try the following meditation exercise:

- Sit in a comfortable position and close your eyes.
- Think of a person who incites anger and pain in you and visualise them sleeping.
- Tell them that you do not hate them anymore.
- Tell them that we're all fallible and they did the best they could at the time.
- Thank them for any positive contribution they've given you, no matter how small.
- Now forgive them.
- Repeat this exercise until you feel your anger and resentment lowering in intensity.

The sooner you rid yourself of the hurt and anger, the sooner you can bring in love.

Remember: Forgiveness is something we decide to do when we are ready to move on. It is a deliberate and voluntary act, but when we choose to forgive we must do it unconditionally. Look after your own mental health – let go of the past and set yourself free.

51

GENEROSITY

Be a generous person.

You've probably come into contact with various individuals who are totally out for themselves, not caring a jot about the needs of other people. This type of person is a taker. Takers are selfish, self-absorbed and self-serving; they're always on the lookout for what they can get from other people. They hog as much money, attention, esteem and conversation as possible. Takers endorse themselves zealously and view life as a hard-nosed competition, only helping others if their individual gain exceeds the cost.

Do you think of yourself as a kind person who gives generously? Or do you usually expect something in return? For example, if you invite friends over to lunch or dinner, do you expect the gesture to be reciprocated? As children we're discouraged from allowing people to take advantage of our good nature. Armed with this attitude, we tend to feel used unless we get a payback in some shape or form, so as a result few of us give freely.

Now here's the problem – if all our giving is conditional on getting, we'll forever be concerned about receiving sufficient payback. Generous, compassionate and sincere giving, which is done without any expectation and free from the worry of payback, will make us feel much more relaxed and in harmony with the world.

So how do we develop into authentically generous people?

Appreciate how abundant your life is

When you appreciate how fortunate you are to have everything that you have in your life, you empower yourself to give generously. Get into the habit of thinking about everything you have and everything that's positive in your life. Do this regularly.

Become a giver

Give to others on a regular basis. How small or large the gesture doesn't matter; it's the giving that counts. The more you do this, the more you'll become a 'giver' with few worries about providing for yourself. If you habitually give time, possessions and money, you'll start to benefit from the feel-good factor that goes with helping others.

These are the key characteristics of givers:

- Instead of feeling superior to downgraded factions of our society, they go out of their way to find out what could help the less privileged.
- They're very happy to give far more than they get back in return. They view helping other people as a reward in itself.
- They're generous with their money and time.
- They're happy to share knowledge and will often sacrifice personal recognition for the needs of a group.
- They try to create successful outcomes for as many people as they can.

Being compassionate and generous and thinking of others will help cultivate your happiness in subtle ways. When you offer someone a gift that they truly appreciate, it produces a mini 'high' within you – a short but powerful feeling of joy. A study by The Ascent also found:

- Generous people report being more satisfied with life and happier than less generous people.
- Generous people are more likely to believe that life is more meaningful, to be optimistic and to be proud of who they are.
- Generous people have closer relationships and more friends.
- Generous people are happier with every aspect of their job and career.

- Positive measures of mental and physical health are also correlated with being generous.

Remember: True generosity comes from a genuine willingness to help people by giving your time, expertise, wisdom or money. Give thanks and praise, and give love without trying to change people. Make a long-lasting commitment – create a pattern of behaviour and form habits that ensure that you keep giving. Society hugely benefits from happy, optimistic and big-hearted givers. These people are inspirational.

If you give regularly and willingly, you'll have a feeling of bonding with people, and a feeling of satisfaction and self-fulfilment that all the money in the world cannot buy.

52

GRATITUDE

Be thankful for all you have.

One of the most widespread and damaging inclinations of modern society is to focus on getting what we don't have rather than appreciating what we already have. No matter how much abundance we already have, we convince ourselves that acquiring more is always better, so we keep on extending our shopping list of requirements. We're not rich enough, not attractive enough, our house isn't big enough, our car isn't new enough and so it goes on. We're perpetually dissatisfied because when we do get what we want, we simply want more. We'll never find happiness when we're always longing for new things.

The way to change this mindset is to focus on the things we do have; cherish them, enjoy them and be grateful for them.

Develop a thankful attitude

Many people in the world, especially the Third World, have less than you. A lot less. So begin to appreciate and value what you have. Rather than wishing you had a better car, just be grateful for the one you have. Only 18 per cent of people in the world own a car. Imagine what your life would be like without one. Instead of focusing on what your partner lacks, be thankful for all the good things he or she brings into your life.

If you make a habit of thinking about everything there is to be grateful for, you're likely to get more of what you want, simply because your mind will be rewired toward what's positive about your life rather than what's negative.

With a thankful outlook, you'll find joy in ordinary moments, such as hugging a loved one, enjoying a glass of wine with good food, or just being outside on a beautiful day. You'll learn to appreciate your freedom, your health, your house, even the tap that delivers hot and cold water. If you live in an affluent country, you're unlikely to fully appreciate these things because you take them for granted. But for millions of people on this planet, these basic things don't exist. Look at your own life from the perspective of someone living in the Third World. Someone whose children don't have a school to go to and without access to a modern hospital. Someone with barely enough money to feed their family.

Practise poverty

Try This: A useful gratitude exercise is to visualise not having certain things. When loading the dishwasher, imagine doing the dishes by hand. When you get into your car, imagine how you'd get to your destination without it. When you buy something, no matter how small, imagine not having the money to buy it.

You can take this thought exercise even further. Rather than just visualising the lack of certain things, why not try abstaining from them? In Roman times, a well-known Stoic called Seneca called this 'practising poverty'. You could, for example, wash those dishes by hand or get to a particular destination without a car. Take a shower or bath without hot water. Wash and dry your clothes without a washing machine or dryer. This will help you fully appreciate all those simple things that you normally take for granted.

Try abstaining from certain pleasures occasionally, such as your regular morning coffee or a food you love or your favourite tipple. Hopefully, you'll be more appreciative when you return to it.

Show your appreciation

It's easy to forget many of the little things and many of the people we should be grateful for, so make an effort to express gratitude whenever you get the opportunity. Gratitude isn't just about saying thanks for the sake of politeness; it's about really appreciating people. Expressions of gratitude range from a simple 'thank you', to a thank you letter or maybe a thank you gift. However you choose to express your thanks, regular expressions of gratitude will help everyone around you to feel a little more valued.

Reflect on paper

Try This: You could reinforce the habit of giving thanks by making regular entries in a gratitude journal. Typing, or using a good old-fashioned pen and paper, gives you the time and space to pause and reflect on the wonderful things and wonderful people in your life. When you're feeling sad or disillusioned, open your journal and remind yourself of some of the wonderful things you are grateful for.

Thank your previous self

Try This: All of the good things we have now are the result of what we have done previously in our lives. Think about all the work you have done, the money you have earned, the sacrifices and decisions you have made, which have all led to where you are now. Why not write a letter to your previous self, thanking your previous self for all of the great things he or she has done to get you to where you are now? Include as much detail as you have time to write and come back to it often. While this chapter is about extending gratitude out into the world, it's also important to offer gratitude to yourself.

Try This: You could also write a message of thanks to someone else. This could be a friend, someone who has helped you out, or even someone you don't know – a writer, an actor, a celebrity, a sportsperson or someone else you admire. The point is to steer your mind toward appreciation, and the process of composing the message will do exactly that – even if you don't send it!

A few sentences will usually be sufficient. For example:

Dear Emily,

Thank you for standing by my side when times get hard. Thank you for making me laugh when I didn't even want to smile. Thank you so much for being a good friend – it's a privilege to have you in my life. I hope you have a great day.

A day to be grateful

When observing the world and our surroundings, we only notice the things that we're looking out for. If we look for eyesores and other things that appear less than perfect, we'll spot plenty of them. If we want to find the imperfections of people and organisations, we'll easily find them.

Try This: If you have a tendency to do this, try to flip your mindset for just one day. For a 24-hour period, look out for the amazing things that exist in our world: the wonder of outer space, the incredible miracle and beauty of the natural world, the marvel of mankind's greatest creations and innovations. When you're mindful of the wonderful world around us and how lucky you are, then seemingly commonplace things add value to your life each and every day.

Remember: Happiness doesn't need to be a consequence of random events. By practising gratitude, we can proactively *choose* to be happy. If you move through the day with gratitude as a lifestyle choice, it's hard to feel anything but harmony and goodwill. Appreciation and gratitude for the gifts that life, people and the world have given you will enrich your life beyond compare. Make gratitude your superpower!

53

GUILT

Does your guilt help or hinder you?

Can you define the feeling of guilt? How does it make you feel? Generally speaking, there are two kinds of guilt:

- **Helpful guilt** can be a very useful emotion. It reminds us that we're conscientious, that we care and that we can do better next time around.

- **Unhelpful guilt** causes needless anxiety over things that just aren't our fault. It can cause distress, embarrassment and worry, and lead us to avoid certain people or situations in order to hide or minimise the guilt.

Helpful guilt

Helpful guilt is usually reasonable and balanced, and it helps us grow and learn from our mistakes. It's the emotion you get when you behave improperly: when you wrong someone or create an issue that shouldn't have occurred. This emotion encourages you to modify your conduct and to put things right.

Here's how to handle a situation when you feel helpful guilt:

- **Take responsibility.** Admit the error of your ways and apologise unreservedly – no ifs or buts. Don't attempt to substantiate your wrongdoing or blame it on other people or other circumstances.
- **Right those wrongs.** Either modify your behaviour or put things right, or both.
- **Let go of the guilt.** Acknowledge what has happened and move on. If you find yourself deliberating over the guilt for too long, take a moment to imagine how you would judge the situation if someone else had done what you've done. Do you really deserve the internal lectures that you're giving yourself?

Unhelpful guilt

Unhelpful guilt can make you feel guilty even though you have no influence over a situation or when you've done nothing wrong; for example, when you get something that other people don't have, such as a promotion or a new car. This guilt is groundless and is unhelpful for all parties.

Avoid exposing yourself to this form of guilt by being:

- Realistic about what you can and can't influence.

- Aware that you're only accountable for your actions and not for the thoughts and actions of other people.

Perfectionists tend to set themselves and others ridiculously high benchmarks, so don't allow these people to expose you to disproportionate pressure. Also be wary of those who use emotional blackmail to make you feel guilty in order to control your behaviour: for example, a boss who asks you to work over the weekend 'for the good of the company' and hints that anyone pursuing a healthy work-family equilibrium is not loyal enough to the company. Be politely assertive in these circumstances because the other person is at fault, not you.

Lingering guilt

If your guilt loiters around for too long, it might make it difficult to function normally in your everyday life. For example, you may become very sensitive and unable to make an obvious decision for fear of it being wrong in the eyes of others. To avoid any feelings of guilt, you might begin to ignore your own needs and feel like you have to please everyone. At its extreme, your guilt will cause worry and misery because it makes you over-conscientious.

There are many life situations that might cause us to feel guilty. For example, a working mother might feel guilty for not spending what she believes to be enough time with her child. On the flip side, a working mother on maternity leave might feel guilty for not spending enough time at work. A victim of child abuse may feel guilty if they think they're at fault and therefore responsible for the abuse. The guilt resulting from child abuse can be so overpowering that a victim begins to define themselves by their abuse, which causes huge problems in later life.

Extreme guilt stemming from a mistake you've made may cause you to feel undeserving of happiness, but always remember that your guilt won't undo your mistake, and nor will it make other people's lives better; it just creates a more miserable situation for you. Where appropriate, ask for forgiveness and get on with your life. Also ask yourself for forgiveness. (See Chapter 50 for more on forgiveness.)

If your guilt is causing you to feel stress, anxiety or depression and it's more than you can handle, don't hesitate to speak to a professional counsellor. Counsellors can provide specific exercises that will help you process your emotions. For example, you could keep a daily guilt journal. By writing down how you feel each day, you can monitor and learn more about how your guilt is affecting you. Every day, you could ask yourself this question: 'What can I do today to show myself that I'm worthy of being happy?'

Remember: Always remember that nobody is perfect, nor should they be – imperfection is a side effect of being human. We all make mistakes and we're all just trying our best to navigate our way through the complexities of life. While a little introspection is helpful, don't overthink your mistakes or keep punishing yourself

– instead, fast forward to that moment when you decide to put it behind you and move on.

54

SCHADENFREUDE

How do you react to other people's misfortune?

Have you ever felt good only because someone else feels bad? There's no English word for this celebration of misery, so we use the German word *schadenfreude* (pronounced *SHAH-den-froy-da*). *Schaden* means destruction or harm and *freude* means happiness or liking.

Schadenfreude is within us and to varying degrees within everyone else, although we're normally too embarrassed to admit it. We experience it with friends and acquaintances, and in sports, politics and celebrity scandals – we feel schadenfreude whenever we feel a pang of enjoyment over someone else's misfortune. But is this something we should feel guilty about? Should we be worrying that our gratification at someone else's misfortune might diminish the compassion we also feel for them?

In the spirit of this book, the theoretical answer to these questions is probably yes, but having said that, it's still possible to experience genuine concern and empathy for a friend at the same time as you experience schadenfreude. Humans possess a level of emotional flexibility which is more complicated than adhering to a strict morality. Schadenfreude is an authentic reaction and it's mostly inoffensive. It makes us feel better when we're feeling inferior, and it reminds us that we all fail from time to time. It might even provide us with a little injection of superiority, which could just give us the confidence to press on with a new venture.

Try This: Analyse your own moments of schadenfreude and ask yourself:

- What prompted it?
- Does that person deserve it? If so, why?
- Are you jealous of that person?
- Were they making you feel inferior or incompetent, and if so, why?

Noticing your own moments of schadenfreude and analysing the underlying feelings will help you understand yourself and your own vulnerabilities.

We occasionally feel the world is relentlessly seeking perfection and our flaws and mistakes are something to be eliminated. Schadenfreude paints a different picture, one of satisfaction and liberation that can be found in other people's slip-ups. It's a nod to our vulnerability and our desire to belong. What cheers us up when we hear about someone else's adversity is the realisation that we're not alone in our setbacks and that we're part of a society of flawed human beings.

55

PARENTING

A very imperfect science!

My wife and I have two girls (aged nine and eleven at the time of writing). We've read a few books and articles on parenting, and yet we'd both agree that it's very difficult to get it right all of the time. Most child psychologists would also agree with us because children vary greatly in their emotional and behavioural patterns, their personalities, their intelligence, their likes and dislikes, their learning methods, their creativity, their music and sporting abilities, their sense of humour, etc. And just when you think you've worked them out, they grow a little older and reinvent themselves.

This subject is deserving of a book in its own right, but I will limit the material here to some key takeaways which you'll hopefully find useful.

Adjusting to parenthood

Being a parent is a challenging undertaking, and after the euphoria of welcoming a newborn baby into the family, some new parents find that parenthood can have a negative effect on their relationship.

- Sleep is usually disrupted, so tiredness has a major influence on everyone's mood.
- The increased workload due to childcare and extra domestic chores can be overwhelming and not all parents share the load fairly, leading to potential conflict.
- Parents have diverse attitudes to giving themselves time off from childcare. Typically, fathers are more able to take a break and unwind, whereas mothers often feel guilty about allocating time to themselves instead of their child, which leads to differences of opinion.
- Each parent needs to get used to no longer being the number one person in their partner's life.

From underparenting to overparenting

Different parents have different attitudes to parenting, ranging from extreme underparenting to extreme overparenting. Most children benefit from a happy medium, but it's worth noting what the extremes look and feel like so you can avoid them.

Underparenting is characterised by those parents who take very little interest in their child and care little for their educational and emotional needs. These parents are borderline negligent, and their child can become unruly or streetwise at a very young age, leading to high levels of antisocial behaviour.

At the other end of the spectrum, overparenting is usually driven by a mistrust in the education system and society as a whole. These parents see the world as a dangerous place, and they view their child's school as fundamentally flawed. They make numerous attempts to interfere with their child's schooling and they become excessively involved in all aspects of the child's life. They're obsessed with their kid's test scores, with their sporting achievements and with the plethora of extracurricular activities that are available.

Problems occur when parents take care of everything, resulting in the child failing to become self-reliant and failing to gain the self-confidence that goes with it. Children need to acquire rudimentary life skills such as how to organise homework and deadlines, how to converse with different types of people and how to fail. Their future employers want to recruit someone who can assess situations, work independently and meet deadlines – qualities that are often lacking when a person has been over parented.

Overparenting also creates unrealistic expectations for the child. The parent's ego manifests itself in the child and they perceive everything the child does, from how they dress to how they behave and perform, as a reflection of them. The parent refrains from talking about their own failings and insecurities, preferring to talk only about their accomplishments. The child then thinks they have to live up to the parent's idealistic expectations, and they find this overwhelming.

Overparenting is also bad for the parents themselves. They're so consumed with ensuring that their plan for the kids is so perfect that they frequently feel tired and worried in case there is something else they should be doing.

Balanced parents

This is how parenting looks when you're a balanced parent:

- You set high expectations but allow your child the freedom to fail and to learn from these failures (see the later section 'Learning from mistakes').
- You don't let the child avoid responsibility or blame others for their mistakes, but ensure they face the consequences of their actions.
- You set clear boundaries backed up with consequences for any digressions, at the same time being receptive to your child's needs.
- You give the child autonomy to make some of their own decisions and experiment.

- You explain the logic behind setting boundaries, so that the child understands why they exist.

Newborn babies enter the world wanting to explore and learn and this mindset should be encouraged and nurtured. Give your child the freedom to discover the world and make mistakes, but don't forget that you're in charge, so if your son or daughter does something wrong, you will need to tell them off and explain exactly why you are telling them off. If you threaten a certain consequence for specific bad behaviour, then be sure to follow through with that consequence, otherwise your child will soon realise they can get away with it.

Structure

Young children need simplicity and regularity in their daily routine because it provides a stable platform from which to explore and learn. Breakfast, lunch, dinner, bathtime and bedtime need to follow a repeated schedule every day, free of disruptions and insecurity.

Praise

Some parents like to praise their kids whenever the opportunity arises, but consider how this praise is perceived by the child. There are types of praise that can be helpful and types of praise that can actually be harmful.

Stanford psychology professor Carol Dweck has conducted research into the impact of diverse praising styles. She found that children who were praised for being intelligent were excessively concerned with how clever they were, and to maintain their status of being 'intelligent', they gravitated toward tasks that would prove their intelligence and avoided tasks that might not. These children also believe that if they have the ability, they shouldn't have to try hard. As a result, they were far less likely to persevere with more challenging tasks than students who were praised for being 'hardworking'.

Praising children for their effort and the processes they use – engagement, perseverance, strategising, self-improvement – fosters motivation, increased effort, willingness to take on new challenges, greater self-confidence and a higher level of success. So when your child gets a good test score, instead of telling them how clever they are, praise the effort they put into preparing for the test.

Learning from mistakes

When children understand that their talents can improve with hard work, determination and persistence, they fear failure much less. As I explain in Chapter 26, failure is an experience we all need to help us develop and move forward. But some parents deny their children the freedom to fail. When a parent constantly intervenes and prevents their child making mistakes, they're subconsciously telling the child that they're incapable and that failure is unacceptable. If you allow your child to fail, however, you're providing them with the freedom they need to independently develop new proficiencies while boosting their self-esteem.

Free play

As part of their ongoing development, try to cultivate curiosity, responsibility and independence while allowing your child to be a child. Free play is very important and should be random, unprompted by parents and based solely on the child's preferences. Encourage your child to play outside. Children who play outdoors tend to play more imaginatively and develop more independence than those who rarely go outside.

Also, if children are constantly given new playthings, there's a risk that they'll end up having too many things to choose from. When a child's play area is crammed full of toys, playtime just revolves around physical objects and doesn't encourage creative and resourceful free play.

The American Academy of Paediatrics (AAP) recommends that no child under the age of 18 months should get any screen time and that young children above this age should only watch a small amount, preferably with their caregiver.

Getting your child involved in sports and other fun things is generally good for them but try not to fill your child's timetable with too many activities. Children will only put maximum energy into what really interests them so be selective. For various reasons, including a fear of missing out, some parents drag their child along to every child activity that's available. Unfortunately, this often leads to tiredness and leaves little or no downtime to fully engage in the creative free play that's highly important for their development.

To intervene or not to intervene?

While parents are important role models, kids learn their social skills mostly through interaction with other kids. When they play, children learn to communicate with each other, teach each other, negotiate with each other and collaborate. While they develop empathy by observing the impact of their words and actions on other kids, there will be times when parents need to intervene and talk to their children about their behaviour, especially if they're being unkind to other children. It's all part of the learning process.

Family contributions

Encouraging your child to do housework helps them learn perseverance, competence, autonomy, accountability and the importance of contribution. They feel trusted and useful. This will help them to become self-motivated and self-sufficient in later life. It's useful to label housework as 'a family contribution' so children feel they are a valued member of the family team. Delegating household jobs isn't just to do with getting those jobs done; it's also to do with family bonding.

Young children are usually keen to get involved, but they often lack the basic skills and coordination, so parents are tempted to take over. If you do this, you're effectively telling them you think their contribution is of no value, so be patient, give some basic guidance and they'll eventually find a way of doing it. It's critical for a child's self-image that their carers have confidence in their capabilities and allow them to do things, even if progress is slow at the start.

Rewards

To induce their kids to do more work around the house or to work hard for exams, many parents offer cash or gifts as an incentive. This is okay in small doses, but overuse of external rewards inhibits a child's self-motivation to get the work done. The more you allow your children to decide for themselves how, when and where they do their work, without expecting financial rewards or material goods as an incentive, the more you nurture their independence and self-motivation.

Schoolwork

Encouraging your child to be independent in carrying out tasks doesn't mean you don't have a say in the matter. Feel free to set homework deadlines, but remember the work itself belongs to your child, so exclude yourself from the task unless your help is requested. If you do help, focus on encouraging the child to discover different ways of solving problems themselves.

Emotional support

Most parents want their children to be happy. In the real world, however, they're unlikely to be happy all of the time, yet many parents try to question the validity of their kid's unhappiness. They're so bemused and annoyed by their kid's negative emotions that they direct them toward expressing only positive emotions. They reject their child's feelings of rage, worry, unhappiness and envy, resulting in the child concealing or suppressing these feelings.

Experiencing negative emotions is a normal and expected part of childhood, and it's the parents role to help their child work their way through these emotions. Make sure you start by listening, understanding and letting the child know it's okay that they feel the way they do. Then help your child work through the problem by themselves rather than attempting to fix it for them. As they get older you'll be less and less able to manipulate the world around them, so focus on nurturing various coping mechanisms. They'll then be better equipped to find their own solutions when you're not around.

Try This: Here's a useful exercise. Just before bedtime, ask your child to tell you about two or three things that they liked about their day and why. Was it because they tried their best and the teacher noticed, or because they finally understood the latest science topic or simply because they had a great time with their friends? If they learn to look back and identify how their actions created these enjoyable outcomes, it will motivate them to re-enact these actions again and again.

Foster empathy, kindness and gratitude

Empathy doesn't come naturally to children, so parents need to show them how to express empathy in a variety of scenarios. The first stage is for parents to express empathy themselves by acknowledging their child's opinions and emotions and making sure the child sees that their thoughts and feelings are understood and taken seriously. Parents then need to show their children how to express empathy whilst interacting with their peers and other people they come into contact with.

Try This: Each evening, ask your child to think of an act of kindness that they can do the following day and then encourage them to go ahead and do it. The following evening, ask your child to describe how it went and how it made them feel. This exercise will hopefully underline how little acts of kindness and compassion can make their child, as well as other people, a little bit happier.

Also, encouraging gratitude in your child will help them recognise all the ways in which other people improve their lives. Help them to keep a gratitude journal of all the things they're thankful for on a daily basis.

The teenage years

If you thought the early years of parenting were tough, wait until those hormones start to kick in! So what happens when a child becomes an adolescent?

Risk-taking behaviour

Largely due to an underdeveloped frontal cortex, an adolescent's behaviour is characterised by thoughtlessness, recklessness and impetuosity. Previously doting youngsters now find their parents embarrassing. Teenagers are subconsciously getting ready to go it alone, and being rude to their parents is one way for them to simulate emotional detachment. By experimenting with life and prioritising their friends over their family, adolescents are preparing themselves for life as independent adults.

They often know the trouble they'll get into, but that doesn't prevent poor behaviour because at this age they love to challenge authority and test boundaries. Dopamine, which produces an immediate and pleasurable response when we engage in exciting or risky activities, spikes during adolescence. This goes some way to explain why teenagers give in to their impulses – they're on the lookout for the next dopamine 'high'.

Parents sometimes react by taking the line of least resistance, treating their teenager like an adult and allowing them to make their own choices. The logic here is that when their teenage child has got it out of their system, they'll be more calm and less restless. However, parents need to remain engaged in order to help their child manage the risks. Parents must prevent their teenager from going too far and from coming to any harm. Discipline is also still important and standards of behaviour need to be maintained. Even for adolescents, discipline is still a key part of the growing up process.

Social bonds

As they become more independent, teenagers search out new support structures and deeper social-bonding experiences with their friends. Adolescents want to belong to their peer group, but inexperience and lack of confidence can sometimes make them feel uncomfortable and inadequate. Parents can help by encouraging their teenage child to speak freely. Anything and everything they feel, think or observe – their aspirations, relationship difficulties, love, sex – should be allowed to come out. Their thoughts and feelings aren't always rational, but they are real, so be patient and focus heavily on listening – offer advice sparingly because teenagers ultimately need to fix their own problems.

Differing opinions

In their quest for independence, adolescents not only distance themselves from older generations; they also begin to think more innovatively. As they become more worldly, they search for their own answers to societal problems. It can sometimes be challenging for parents to fully agree with their teenager's opinions, but it's important to listen carefully to them rather than simply overruling them. Once again, be patient – they'll work it out eventually.

Let your child discover their own journey

Rather than overprotecting your children, allow them to experiment and experience the world using their own initiative. Children develop their own interests and aspirations, and they aren't put on Earth to follow a route that was mapped out by other people. As a parent, you need to allow your child to find out who they truly are and find their own life journey.

Time for you

Some parents live solely for their kids, often forgetting about their own needs and desires. Adults and children have different interests and different needs, so it's perfectly okay to allocate some time for yourself and your partner. Don't feel like you have to go to every sports match and don't be hesitant about using a babysitter or sending your child on a sleepover. They'll have a great time and it will allow you to disengage, rest and unwind. As a role model, it's useful to show your kids that you also love to have fun and spend time with your friends.

Don't compare

Parents often get caught up in comparisons with other families. They can feel insecure about their parenting style, worrying that they're too harsh or too soft. Parenting is a learning process that's different for every family, so just keep learning and above all else, trust yourself.

Remember: Most parents feel their children are importance sources of life satisfaction, but parenthood does come with a tremendous amount of responsibility, sprinkled with a pinch of additional stress. Speaking for my wife and I, the benefits of parenthood outweigh the hardships because our children bring much joy, purpose, meaning and fulfilment to our lives.

56

CONTROL

Do you need to be in control?

One of the key characteristics of successful people is a conviction that they have control over their own destiny. They believe that they can organise and manage their career, relationships and lifestyle. These individuals take responsibility for their own personal development and are accountable for their own achievements or failures. A feeling of control is a great motivational force and a big contributor to personal happiness.

This is straightforward positive psychology, but there's one major caveat: if your success and happiness depend heavily on the outcomes of things you can't control, you run the risk of being let down, leading to lower enthusiasm and self-confidence, and ultimately, unhappiness. The need to be able to control our environment is rooted in fear – the fear of what might happen outside our control.

Focus on what you can control

In an ideal world we would all feel in control of every aspect of our lives. Unfortunately, we don't live in an ideal world and our lives don't always go as planned, so if we have too many predetermined and inflexible thoughts about the way our lives ought to be, it interferes with our ability to enjoy the life we actually have. For example, virtually all of us want things that we can't get. That's a normal part of life, but problems occur when we let it bother us if we don't get these things. Fighting against things that you can't control is not only futile, it causes unnecessary stress.

Clearly, then, we need to separate the things we can control from those we can't, and focus on finding joy and fulfilment from a multitude of different outcomes. It isn't always easy, but we need to claim ownership of our own happiness and stop blaming other people or circumstances out of our control for how we feel. For example, you have full control over the values you live by, such as by becoming an honest, happy, dependable and compassionate person, but you can't exercise control over the values and actions of other people. This doesn't mean that you need to be less ambitious, just fully grounded in life's realities. As you push forward with your goals, you'll gain experience and build confidence, while being philosophical when people let you down or things go wrong.

Try This: For any given project or issue, it might be useful to make a list of things you can control and a list of things you can't control. Now approach your two lists as follows:

- Can any of your 'can't control' items be moved over to the 'can control' list by tweaking your strategy? You might need to think creatively here.
- Make sure you're fully aware of the consequences of the possible outcomes of the 'can't control' items. Make contingency plans where appropriate.
- Now forget that list and put all of you energy into your 'can control' list.

At this stage, it might be useful to rework some of your goals so that you're aiming for things a little more within your control. For example, in a sporting competition you have no control over the opponent and therefore the result, so your goal could be to prepare as best you can, stick to your game plan and enjoy yourself. When you concentrate on your effort and your capabilities, instead of the result, you're likely to put in a better performance anyway.

Remember: If you're one of those people who only feels content when they have complete control over their ecosystem and the people in it, you're setting yourself up for failure. We can never be in complete control and when it comes to other people, we shouldn't want to control them anyway. You most likely don't enjoy being controlled by others, so it's highly likely that other people won't enjoy being controlled by you.

57

AWE

Enrich your life with the ultimate experiences.

Picture yourself standing on the rim of the Grand Canyon in the USA. The canyon sweeps out before you for miles and miles in all directions and it is much wider and deeper than you had expected. In that moment, as you stare out at that extraordinary, breathtaking and enormous vista, you feel as though you've become spiritually connected to the planet. You feel an immense sense of awe.

What inspires awe?

Awe is often stimulated by sheer size, like the ocean, a huge lake, high mountains or the pyramids. The feeling can also be stimulated by a live performance, or it can be theoretical, such as imagining the vastness of the universe. We also feel awe when we have a profound experience, such as being in the presence of someone you hold in high esteem or discovering an insightful idea like the theory of relativity.

Benefits of awe

Any experience that gives us an intensified sense of magnificence, marvel, delight or tranquillity boosts our spiritual well-being. Awe-inspiring experiences move our attention away from ourselves and make us feel like we're part of something greater. We feel open and curious, which encourages personal growth in other areas of our life.

Being filled with awe is a wonderful feeling and it positively affects our state of mind such that we:

- Have increased sense of fulfilment
- Are less aggressive
- Have more enthusiasm and drive
- Build more fulfilling relationships
- Have less fear of death
- Are more generous toward others
- Demonstrate good critical thinking
- Feel more positive
- Are less focused on materialism

Find your awe

The simple act of recalling an awe-filled experience in vivid detail can be very powerful. Even just a brief reminder of an awe-inspiring experience from the past might help raise your spirits and remind you that the world can be an enchanting and wonderful place.

Try This: To generate more awe-inspiring experiences, treat your surroundings as if you're seeing or hearing them for the first time. Maybe even look upwards a little more? In this way, a bird's song, the colour of the sky, a beautiful cloud formation or a previously unnoticed tree might be transformed into something extraordinary.

With the right outlook, we can find awe in many places, converting seemingly commonplace scenery into a source of inspiration and wonder. These could include natural settings, like a hiking trail lined with tall trees, or urban settings, like at the top of a skyscraper or a historic building.

You're more likely to feel awe in new places, where the sights and sounds are unfamiliar to you. So go and seek out new experiences and see where they take you. As they stir humility, curiosity and wonder within, you might just discover that they act as a signpost toward what you're supposed to do while you're here on Earth.

58

DEATH

Do you think about your own death?

Unlike all other animals on Earth, humans think about death. We think of our own death as well as those around us. With that in mind, we think about and carefully plan how we're going to spend our short time on this planet. Our contemplation of death also creates an element of fear. We are frightened of our own death and the death of those we love the most. We are frightened of what death means – what is like to not exist anymore?

Throughout history, religion has offered salvation from these fears through beliefs that imply there is another place for us after we die. But as we evolve into less religious times, many of us alleviate our fear of dying by creating a 'historical self' that will survive us as our legacy after death. This incentivises some individuals to pursue notoriety via the arts, sports, entertainment, religion or government. Most people's legacies are positive, but an insatiable desire for immortality can cause warfare, devastation and despair

367

when powerful, destructive leaders attempt to rearrange the world to their own specification.

Contemplate death

Have you ever visualised your own funeral? Most of us occasionally catch ourselves thinking about our own death – maybe the act of dying itself, or our funeral, or how the world looks without us in it. Most of us aren't going to die soon, but we're very aware that at some point in the future we simply won't exist anymore. This type of speculation is likely to make us uncomfortable because death is scary and shadowy – the ultimate journey into the unknown.

However, thinking and talking about death can make it less frightening. One study of funeral directors found that people who had attended more funerals were less anxious about death than those who had attended fewer funerals. Reflecting on your own death can also add context to your life while you're still living. We sometimes focus on our future so much that we don't think about enjoying where we are now. Thinking about our death often stimulates philosophical questions, such as what in our lives brings fun, joy and satisfaction. This contemplation gives us an opportunity to make adjustments to our lives or begin work on that bucket list before it's too late.

Try This: When you meditate, think about your own impermanence, whilst remembering that all things are ultimately impermanent. By reflecting on the process of death while you're healthy, when your time eventually does arrive, you'll be better placed to pass away without distress and with fewer regrets. Rather than being morose, this thought exercise can be very healthy. It keeps you see the big picture and clear out the pettiness in your life. Knowing that your time on this planet is finite will motivate you to live your life. It reminds you to be your best self and to appreciate all the moments in your life. We all lead better lives when we're at peace with the prospect of our own death.

A final word: if you try this, please do not overly obsess about it. While thinking about death is generally healthy, fixating on it for too long is not. Life is essentially for living; right here, right now.

59

CONTENTMENT

Learn to be happy with what you have.

According to Dr Michael McGee, contentment is being happy with who we are, with the people in our lives, and with our life situation. Contentment allows us to enjoy and savour the wonderful gift of existence without the need for something more or something different.

Embrace your uniqueness

Be honest with yourself – are you a jealous person? The truth is, we all experience jealousy to some degree. People usually equate success with acquiring more and as a result we spend our lives pursuing a better lifestyle, accumulating possessions and wanting what others have. From time to time, virtually everyone will make comparisons between themselves and other people. Problems occur, however, when these comparisons are based on criteria and standards we can't realistically live up to. Such comparisons trigger a fear deep inside of not having enough and not being enough.

There are always going to be people in this world who are more prosperous, knowledgeable, gifted, flamboyant or more eye-catching than us, and if we benchmark our success against these people, we'll perpetuate the feeling of not being good enough. And why compare our lives to others' when we have no idea what their journey is all about? Such unrealistic comparisons are unhealthy, so instead we need to proactively embrace and honour ourselves for who we are. We are surrounded by a large number of very different people, each one doing their own thing in their own way.

Life's not fair

Some people spend a lot of time feeling sorry for themselves, constantly grumbling about how unfair everything is. In reality life isn't fair; it's random. We're born into a random place and a random society, and with random strengths, weaknesses and challenges. By accepting the fact that life, due to this randomness, is unfair, we can ditch the self-pity and do the best we can with who we are, where we are and what we have.

But always remember that while life isn't fair, it can still be very good!

Happy with what you have

Why do you think some people spend big money on high-end cars and other showy possessions, even when they don't necessarily need them? It's often because this 'conspicuous consumption' advertises the owner's prosperity and their higher social status.

Pursuing happiness by chasing after money and possessions is commonly perceived as normal, but in reality our mindset influences our happiness far more than our wealth. The world after all, is full of wealthy yet wholly unhappy people. Being blessed with a high degree of wealth isn't immoral or detrimental, but the constant desire for more is ultimately counterproductive.

When we get a new possession or achieve a goal, most of us simply go on to the next possession or the next goal. Psychologists Shane Frederick and George Loewenstein use the term 'hedonic adaption' to describe this behaviour and it follows a typical pattern:

1. We desire a new possession.
2. We buy it and enjoy using it for an initial period of time.
3. Our new possession starts to lose its novelty value and we eventually take it for granted.
4. We search for something novel and superior. The cycle repeats.

We go on to replicate this pattern of behaviour with other items and we become that person who is constantly looking for something better because they are never completely satisfied with what they already have. Compelled by this neurotic habit, we continually strive for the next thing, and the next, and the next, which in the long term just makes us miserable.

So how do we break the cycle? Well, we need to realise that the dissatisfaction doesn't emanate from not having things, but in the *yearning* for those things. We needlessly delay our happiness by fooling ourselves that our lives will be better when this yearning is fulfilled. The fact is, we don't actually need most of these extra things, so rather than allowing your anxiety about not having enough to dominate your thinking, start accepting that you have enough already.

Manufacture your own happiness

When things don't turn out as planned, rather than being unhappy, the brain will often subconsciously attempt to synthesise happiness for us. Dan Gilbert, author of *Stumbling on Happiness*, tells us that this 'synthetic happiness' is just as genuine and lasting as real happiness. For example, the differences between getting or not getting a new job, staying in a relationship or losing a relationship, passing or not passing an exam and winning or losing a sports match are much smaller than we anticipate because our happiness can be synthesised. Synthetic happiness is what we create when we don't get what we want, and it's every bit as authentic and permanent as the happiness we get when we do get what we want.

Various research also shows that we can't forecast our future levels of happiness accurately: we either overestimate our future happiness or overestimate our future unhappiness. For example, we overestimate that having more money will increase our happiness, or we overestimate that having less money will decrease our happiness. Also, when we have a choice, we worry about making the right one, but when we don't have a choice, we grow to like what we've been given due to synthetic happiness. In short, we can manufacture our own happiness no matter what happens.

Remember: By enjoying and being satisfied with what you have, where you are and who you are, you can experience the joy of living right now.

60

LOVE

Give more love to the world.

What is the meaning of love to you? Freudian psychiatrists believe that after food, water and shelter, love is our foremost human desire.

The need for love

Without love, it's harder to see and appreciate who we are and when this happens, we struggle to accept our limitations and imperfections. We need love and that means we need other people, whether it is a mother, a lover or a close friend. We need that person to value what we do and what we say, we need them to want to spend time with us and give us their loyalty and support. Loving relationships show us that we're not alone; that we're respected, valued and loved.

Giving and receiving love galvanises our collective psyche. Love boosts our self-esteem and makes everything seem so much more vivid and pleasurable. We're more kind and compassionate when we give love to the world.

Love is an action

Some people want to love but don't understand that they need to back this up with loving behaviour. There is a clear distinction between wanting to love and an act of love. If you say to your partner 'I would like to cook for you more often', that is a mere intention to love. If, on the other hand, you say 'Here's a lovely meal I prepared while you were out; I hope you enjoy it', this is an act of love. Love requires both loving intentions and actual effort.

Love without conditions

Aside from a very young infant, it's difficult to love someone without conditions. Our loved ones are fallible humans and at some point they will upset us with a missed deadline, a badly timed comment or some other behaviour that we disapprove of. We get hurt and angry and react by leveraging our love; using it as either a carrot or a stick or both: 'You have to behave the way I want if you want me to love you.'

Most religious belief systems encourage unconditional love because it creates secure, warm and loving feelings for all parties concerned. When you love tenderly and unconditionally you understand and empathise with the other person's situation when they let you down, and as a result you feel less stressed, angry or impatient. Don't demand that people become someone else to receive your love. Love everyone just as they are.

Think loving thoughts

Try This: Do you regularly think loving thoughts about yourself and people in your inner circle? Whenever someone irritates you so much that it negatively affects your entire mood, try taking a few seconds to think of someone you love. Hopefully, these thoughts will evoke a more positive mood within you and keep your cynicism in check. Also try offering a warm and loving attitude to the world at large – including those people who get on your nerves. I know that this is easier said than done, but the more positivity you give out each and every day, the more you'll get back.

How many times have you received a message out of the blue saying, 'This is just a quick note to tell you how much I love you!' How do you think you'd react if someone you care about sent you those words? Wouldn't you feel great? While you can't make people send you loving messages, you can certainly send them to other people. If you're too shy, begin by using slightly less gushy language and build up from there. If you make loving communication a regular habit, you will find that love comes back to you in spades.

Remember: Every loving gesture generates more love from those around you, so if you try to initiate loving communication, other people will follow, and the world will become a slightly better place.

THE FINAL WORD

Put it all together using the power of marginal gains.

Marginal gains simply means that you focus on small improvements in everything you do, one per cent at a time. By making many of these small enhancements, you'll find the compound effect is huge. People love to talk about major breakthroughs in their life, but the truth is that most significant improvements are the sum of all the times when we chose to do things just one per cent better. Aggregating these small gains will hopefully make a big difference to your life.

I hope you feel that buying this book was money well spent. All of the sales proceeds are going to MIND, and if you'd like to make an extra contribution to this wonderful charity, please visit my JustGiving page at www.justgiving.com/fundraising/Bradbury65.

Aside from helping MIND with their great work, the best contribution to the world that this book could make is to help as many people as possible build a life they love and look forward to every day. So please recommend the book to your family, friends and colleagues, and please write an honest review of the book online. I'm genuinely interested in your comments, both good and bad.

I hope you've found the book insightful and I hope you've enjoyed working through it. Remember that your life journey is continuous, so review this book and your notes regularly to make sure you're remaining on track. The mistake a lot of people make is to read a book like this and get motivated, but then as time passes they forget everything and return to how they were. So don't just read the book and put it on the shelf.

If you reread the book a few times, I'm pretty sure that each time you'll find new insights and answers. Or you might discover how many principles from the book you've taken on board. Regularly put your thoughts on paper so you can see the steps you're taking towards the goals you want to achieve. Come back to your notes from time to time when you feel the need for inspiration. Keep focused and don't drift back into old habits that don't serve you well.

When you combine your core values with your vision, you can become an unstoppable force in all aspects of life. So let this book be a catalyst for positive change, the beginning of a great journey where you'll find inspiration to take on challenges and build the life you want to live every day.

Good luck!

C.B.

Lightning Source UK Ltd.
Milton Keynes UK
UKHW011847010922
408192UK00004B/97/J